The UK Air Fryer Cookbook: An XXL Collection of Family Favourites - Quick & Super-Delicious Air Fryer Recipes For Every Day I Breakfast, Lunch, Dinner, Sides, Snacks & More

Hanna Oliver

ISBN: 979-8-3631-8693-6

Contents

EXCLUSIVE BONUS

40 Weight Loss Recipes
&
14 Days Meal Plan

Scan the QR-Code and receive
the FREE download:

INTRODUCTION

Air fryers are far more common than they ever used to be. That means it's possible you've been given an air fryer as a gift or you found a bargain and decided to snap one up. Great choice - air fryers are versatile and have a wealth of benefits too.

Air fryers create delicious meals that are crispy and totally devoid of the high fat content that comes with deep fat frying. You can make all manner of different meals in your new appliance, including snacks and desserts too.

There are many different types of air fryers on the market, so it's important to shop around and find the right choice for you. By following the instructions on the manufacturer's leaflet, you'll notice just how easy air fryers are to use.

An air fryer is also the perfect option for cooking family meals. You can easily add ingredients, quickly follow instructions, and you'll have a delicious and tasty meal for everyone at the end. In most cases, recipes take less than half an hour! That's a major plus point when you have several hungry mouths to feed.

What is an Air Fryer?

If you're not sure what an air fryer is, or you're thinking of buying one and you need to be sure that you're investing in an appliance that is going to do everything you need, this section is for you. An air fryer is a kitchen appliance that cooks food in air. No need for oil. That means your food will be crunchier, healthier, and will taste fresher as a result.

Foods that are cooked in an air fryer have a distinctively home-cooked taste and they're not oily or heavy. As long as you follow the instructions for your particular air fryer, you'll be on the fast-track to delicious food before you know it.

Cooking meals in an air fryer is also very easy because you usually only have to add your ingredients to the appliance in a specific order and follow recipe timings. Then, your food is ready to enjoy!

It's oh-so-easy!

The Benefits of Using an Air Fryer

Of course, there are many kitchen appliances on the market, so you may be wondering why you should invest in another one. Air fryers have many other benefits that make them a worthwhile purchase.

The main benefits of owning and using an air fryer are:

Easy to use

Food is cooked quickly

No need to use large amounts of oil, which makes your creations much healthier

Crispy foods

Easy to store and clean

You can create a huge number of recipes in your air fryer

When purchasing an air fryer, it's important to shop around. There are many different models out there, and you need to make sure that you're purchasing an appliance that is not only within your budget, but one that has the correct capacity and features for you.

A few key things to look for when purchasing an air fryer include:

- **The size of the air fryer** – Some air fryers are larger than others and you should purchase one that suits your needs. It's no good buying an air fryer that is much bigger than you really need. Remember you also need to store your air fryer when not in use, so checking its overall size is important.

- **The cost** – Identify a budget and find an appliance that fits into your price bracket.

- **Brand name and guarantee** – Most people feel happier buying an air fryer from a large brand name because that gives peace of mind from the get-go. You should also check the guarantee you get with the appliance.

- **Number of features** – Some devices have more features than others and the more features it has, the higher the price. Identify the features you need and then look for the appliance that best suits your needs.

Why is an Air Fryer a Great Choice For Families?

These days, we're all far more focused on health and wellbeing but when you have a family to feed, you'll want to make sure that you cover all health-related bases even more. If you have children, you'll want to give them the right vitamins and minerals to make sure they grow and develop correctly. And even if you don't have children, you'll want to feed your family in the healthiest way possible.

An air fryer helps you to do that because you're not cooking in oil. That in itself gives you a fresher and crispier taste to your food. But, we're also cutting down on saturated fat here and that's a major plus point!

An air fryer also saves you a lot of time because you can often simply combine ingredients and then add them to your air fryer in the correct order. It's a far simpler way of creating fantastic meals and snacks for all the family. And, we all know that when you have a family, time is very precious - you're running around all the time and you need to save as many precious minutes as possible!

Using an air fryer is therefore a great appliance to add to a family kitchen.

Air Fryer Maintenance

When you look after your air fryer, it's going to last you longer and you'll run into fewer problems. The good news is that looking after your air fryer isn't rocket science and you simply need to know a few basic rules to make sure that you don't accidentally damage your appliance. That way, it will last you longer than it would otherwise do.

Clean your appliance after every use, making sure you follow the manufacturer's instructions for cleaning your particular model.

Avoid using abrasive cleaning sponges when cleaning your appliance. Instead, a soft cloth will do the job.

When cleaning your fryer, never totally submerge it in water - remember that it is an electric device and that doesn't go well with water!

Never clean your air fryer until it is totally cool and make sure you unplug before cleaning

If you need to dismantle any pieces, make sure they're totally dry before putting the device back together again.

Always remember to follow manufacturer instructions to the letter when operating your air fryer. All models vary slightly and you need to make sure that you're using your appliance as it's supposed to be used. By doing that, you can look forward to a long and happy future with your air fryer by your side!

The best way to get started with your air fryer is to pick one of the delicious recipes we're about to show you throughout the book and then just go for it. Practice makes perfect!

AIR FRYER BREAKFAST RECIPES

Breakfast is the most important meal of the day but that doesn't mean you need to get the frying pan out and start frying everything in oil! Your air fryer has the ability to create some seriously delicious, not to mention healthy, recipes.

Let's check out some fantastic breakfast choices you can make in your new air fryer.

Air Fryer French Toast

SERVINGS - 1

CALORIES - 302, PROTEIN - 3G, FAT - 1G, CARBS - 23G

Ingredients:

- 5 slices of bread - sandwich bread works best
- 2 medium eggs
- 2 tbsp flour
- 3 tbsp white sugar

- 100ml/0.5 cups of milk
- 0.5 tsp vanilla extract
- 1 tsp ground cinnamon
- 0.5 tsp salt

Method:

1. Preheat the air fryer to 220C/390F and place a piece of parchment paper inside
2. Cut each slice of bread into three equal pieces
3. Combine all the other ingredients in a mixing bowl
4. Dip the slices of bread into the mixing bowl, covering all sides
5. Place the bread onto the parchment paper, inside the air fryer
6. Cook for 5 minutes on each side

Burgers For Breakfast

SERVINGS - 2

CALORIES - 402, PROTEIN - 4G, FAT - 3G, CARBS - 21G

Ingredients:

- 8 skinless sausages
- Salt and pepper for seasoning

Method:

1. Preheat your air fryer to 260C/500F
2. Take a bowl and mash up the sausages
3. Add a little salt and pepper and combine again
4. Use your hands to create patties out of the sausage mixture
5. Place the patties into the air fryer cook for 8 minutes

Cheesy "Oven" Eggs

SERVINGS - 2

CALORIES - 303, PROTEIN - 4G, FAT - 2.6G, CARBS - 21G

Ingredients:

- 140g/5oz smoked gouda cheese
- 4 medium eggs
- Salt and pepper for seasoning
- 2 ramekin dishes, sprayed with a little cooking oil

Method:

1. Preheat the air fryer to 350C/650F
2. Cut the cheese into small pieces
3. Crack an egg into each of the ramekin dishes and top with half the cheese in each one
4. Season to your liking and arrange inside the air fryer
5. Cook for 15 minutes, making sure the eggs are to your liking before serving

Vegetable Hash Browns

SERVINGS – 4

CALORIES – 206, PROTEIN – 5G, FAT – 2G, CARBS – 40G

Ingredients:

- 2 tbsp olive oil
- 4 potatoes, grated
- 2 tbsp bicarbonate of soda
- 1 tsp cayenne pepper
- 1 onion, chopped
- 1 red pepper, chopped
- 1 green pepper, chopped
- 1 tbsp salt
- 1 tbsp black pepper

Method:

1. Take a large mixing bowl and fill with water. Add the potatoes
2. Add the bicarbonate of soda and set aside for 30 minutes
3. Preheat the air fryer to 200°C/390F
4. Drain the bowl and remove the potatoes, patting dry, Place them in another bowl
5. Add the oil and the spices to the bowl and combine well
6. Transfer the potatoes to the air fryer basket
7. Cook for 10 minutes
8. Give the potatoes a shake before adding the onions and peppers
9. Cook for a further 10 minutes

Bacon & Mozzarella Toast

SERVINGS – 2

CALORIES – 446, PROTEIN – 21G, FAT – 21G, CARBS – 23G

Ingredients:

- 4 slices of sandwich bread
- 1 tbsp butter, melted
- 5 slices of bacon, cooked

- 2 slices of cheddar cheese
- 2 slices of mozzarella cheese

Method:

1. Spread the butter onto one side of each slice of bread
2. Set the air fryer to 170ºC/330F
3. Place the bread into the fryer, with the buttered side down
4. Place the cheddar on top, the bacon, mozzarella, and top with the other slice of bread. The buttered side should face upwards
5. Cook for 4 minutes
6. Turn over and cook for another 3 minutes

Egg & Ham Cups

SERVINGS – 4

CALORIES – 82, PROTEIN – 4G, FAT – 5G, CARBS –11G

Ingredients:

- 8 slices of sandwich bread, toasted
- Butter for greasing
- 2 slices of ham

- 4 eggs
- Salt and pepper for seasoning
- 4 ramekin dishes, greased

Method:

1. Preheat the air fryer to 160ºC/320F
2. Take a rolling pin and flatten the toast
3. Place two slices of toast into each ramekin
4. Line the inside of each dish with ham
5. Crack one egg into each dish and season
6. Place the ramekins into the air fryer basket and for 15 minutes
7. Cool before serving

Scrambled Eggs With Cheese

SERVINGS – 1

CALORIES – 109, PROTEIN – 9G, FAT – 8G, CARBS – 3.5G

Ingredients:

- 1 tbsp butter
- 2 tbsp milk
- 2 eggs
- 100g/3.5oz cheese, grated
- Salt and pepper for seasoning

Method:

1. Preheat the air fryer to 220C/420F
2. Add the butter and cook until melted
3. Take a bowl and combine the eggs and milk with a little seasoning
4. Pour the mixture into the fryer and cook for 3 minutes, scrambling gently
5. Add the cheese and continue to cook for another 2 minutes

Cheesy Chorizo Frittata

SERVINGS – 2

CALORIES – 401, PROTEIN – 21G, FAT – 24G, CARBS – 16G

Ingredients:

- 1 tbsp olive oil
- 3 eggs
- 1 chorizo sausage, sliced
- 1 boiled potato, cut into cubes
- 50g/1.7oz feta cheese
- 50g/1.7oz sweetcorn
- A pinch of salt

Method:

1. Preheat the air fryer to 180°C/350F
2. Add a little olive oil to the basket and allow to warm up
3. Add the potato, sweetcorn and chorizo
4. Cook until the sausage has browned
5. In a separate bowl, combine the eggs with a little seasoning
6. Pour the mixture into the pan with the crumbled feta on top
7. Cook for 5 minutes
8. Slice before serving

Swiss Cheese Breakfast Sandwich

SERVINGS – 4

CALORIES – 244, PROTEIN – 2G, FAT – 5G, CARBS – 28G

Ingredients:

- 1 egg
- 1 tsp butter, melted
- 2 slices of sandwich bread
- 4 slices of Swiss cheese

- 4 slices of ham
- 4 slices of turkey
- ¼ tsp vanilla extract
- A pinch of powdered sugar

Method:

1. Preheat the air fryer to 220C/420F
2. Combine the egg and vanilla extract in a bowl
3. Take a slice of bread and top with a slice of cheese, then ham, turkey and cheese again, topping with another slice of bread
4. Press the sandwich down
5. Brush a piece of foil with butter
6. Dip your sandwich into the egg mixture and make sure that it's coated on both sides
7. Place it on the foil to rest for a minute
8. Place in the air fryer and cook for 3 minutes
9. Turn over and cook for 3 minutes on the other side
10. Slice before serving

Spicy Breakfast Wrap

SERVINGS - 2

CALORIES - 503, PROTEIN - 2.3G, FAT - 4G, CARBS - 28G

Ingredients:

- 25g/0.8oz cooked pinto beans
- 2 tortillas
- 2 corn tortillas, crushed
- 1 jalapeño pepper, sliced
- 4 tbsp ranchero sauce
- 1 avocado, sliced

Method:

1. Preheat your air fryer to 190°C/370F
2. Take your tortillas and add the jalapeño, ranchero sauce, crushed corn tortillas, avocado, and pinto beans
3. Fold the wrap to make sure all the ingredients stay inside
4. Carefully add each wrap into your fryer and cook for 6 minutes
5. Once cooked, carefully take the wraps out of the air fryer and transfer to the oven
6. Cook at 180°C/350F for another 5 minutes
7. Then, transfer to a frying pan and cook on a low heat to add more crisp. This shouldn't take more than 2 minutes Turn over and do the same to the other side

Fruity Breakfast Muffins

SERVINGS - 12

CALORIES - 310, PROTEIN - 6G, FAT - 7G, CARBS - 52G

Ingredients:

- 2 tbsp of cooking oil
- 2 eggs
- 315g/11oz self-raising flour
- 65g/2oz sugar
- 120ml/0.5 cups of double/heavy cream
- 125g/4.4oz blueberries
- The zest and juice of a lemon
- 1 tsp vanilla

Method:

1. Preheat your air fryer to 150°C/300F
2. Combine the self-raising flour and sugar in a small bowl
3. In a separate bowl, combine the oil, juice, eggs, vanilla, and cream
4. Add the wet mixture to the flour mixture and combine
5. Fold in the blueberries carefully with a plastic spatula
6. Use silicone muffin holders if you have them. Carefully spoon the mixture into the muffin holders
7. Place the muffin holders into the air fryer basket and cook for 10 minutes
8. Check the muffins the halfway point. If they're cooking too fast, turn the heat down
9. Allow to cool before removing from the muffin holders

Stuffed Bell Peppers

SERVINGS - 2

CALORIES - 154, PROTEIN - 10G, FAT - 9G, CARBS - 3G

Ingredients:

- 1 tsp olive oil
- 1 large bell pepper, deseeded and halved
- 4 eggs
- Salt and pepper for seasoning

Method:

1. Preheat your air fryer to 200ºC/390F
2. Rub some of the olive oil onto the edges of the olives
3. Add one egg into each pepper and a little seasoning
4. Create a trivet inside your air fryer basket, so the peppers don't fall over
5. Carefully place the peppers inside
6. Cook for 13 minutes, checking regularly
7. Season once more before serving

Homemade Breakfast Bagels

SERVINGS - 2

CALORIES - 233, PROTEIN - 2G, FAT - 4G, CARBS - 28G

Ingredients:

- 1 egg, beaten
- 170g/6oz self-raising flour
- 120ml/0.5 cups of plain yogurt

Method:

1. Preheat your air fryer to 170°C/330F
2. Combine the flour and the yogurt in a large bowl and create a dough
3. Cover a flat surface some flour and turn the dough out onto the floured surface
4. Divide the dough into four balls, even in size
5. Roll each ball out into a rope shape
6. Form a bagel from the rope shape
7. Brush the beaten egg over each bagel, covering completely to avoid burning
8. Arrange the bagels inside your fryer, keeping them on one layer and avoiding overlaps
9. Cook for 10 minutes
10. Allow to cool completely before serving

Sweet Potato Hash

SERVINGS - 6

CALORIES - 190, PROTEIN - 3G, FAT - 5G, CARBS - 31G

Ingredients:

- 2 tbsp olive oil
- 2 sweet potatoes, cubed
- 1 tbsp smoked paprika
- 2 slices of bacon, chopped
- Salt and pepper for seasoning

Method:

1. Preheat your air fryer to 200°C/390F
2. Take a large mixing bowl and add the olive oil
3. Add the potatoes, bacon, and seasoning. Toss and make sure everything is coated
4. Transfer into the air fryer and cook for 12-16 minutes
5. After 10 minutes, give everything a stir and keep stirring every so often for the next 5 minutes

Berry Pockets

SERVINGS - 1

CALORIES - 255, PROTEIN - 3G, FAT - 5G, CARBS - 30G

Ingredients:

- 1 egg
- 1 tbsp soft cream cheese
- 2 slices of sandwich bread
- 1 tbsp raspberry jam
- 1 tbsp milk

Method:

1. Spray the inside of the fryer with a little oil and preheat the air fryer to 190°C/370F
2. Take one slice of the bread and add a tablespoon of jam into the middle
3. Take another slice of bread and add the cream cheese in the centre again
4. Spread the jam and the cream cheese over the bread but avoid the edges
5. Place one slice of bread over the other to make a sandwich
6. Whisk the eggs and the milk together in a small mixing bowl
7. Dip the sandwich into the egg and carefully place inside your air fryer
8. Cook for 5 minutes before turning and cooking for a further 2 minutes on the other side

Eggs With Gouda

SERVINGS - 2

CALORIES - 393, PROTEIN - 3G, FAT - 4G, CARBS - 21G

Ingredients:

- 4 medium eggs
- 140g/1 cup chopped, smoked gouda cheese
- Salt and pepper for seasoning
- 2 ramekin dishes, sprayed with oil

Method:

1. Crack one egg into each ramekin
2. Add some of the cheese on top of each dish
3. Season to your liking
4. Place the dishes into the air fryer
5. Cook at 350C/660F for 15 minutes

Sweet Apple Pancakes

SERVINGS - 5

CALORIES - 101, PROTEIN - 3G, FAT - 2G, CARBS - 20G

Ingredients:

- 3 large eggs
- 140ml/1 cup milk
- 130g/1 cup of flour
- 2 tbsp apple sauce
- Salt for seasoning
- 5 ramekin dishes

Method:

1. Preheat your air fryer to 200C/390F
2. Spray the ramekins with a little oil and place inside the fryer
3. Combine all ingredients in a blender until smooth
4. Divide the batter between the ramekins
5. Cook for 8 minutes

Jalapeño & Avocado Wrap

SERVINGS - 2

CALORIES - 503, PROTEIN - 2G, FAT - 5G, CARBS - 20G

Ingredients:

- jalapeño pepper, sliced finely
- 1 avocado, sliced
- 2 flour tortillas
- 2 corn tortillas, crushed
- 4 tbsp ranchero sauce
- 25g/0.2 cups of pinto beans, cooked

Method:

1. Top each tortilla with ranchero sauce, jalapeño, crushed corn tortillas, avocado and beans
2. Fold the wraps over securely
3. Place in the air fryer and cook at 190/370F for 6 minutes
4. Once cooked, place your wraps in the oven for 5 minutes, cooking at 180C/350F to crisp a little before serving

Breakfast Sausage Pie

SERVINGS – 4

CALORIES – 406, PROTEIN – 12G, FAT – 30G, CARBS – 27G

Ingredients:

- 4 eggs
- 1 sheet of puff pastry
- 4 tbsp cheddar cheese, grated
- 4 slices of cooked ham, chopped

Method:

1. Preheat the air fryer to 200C/390F
2. Cut the puff pastry into four equal pieces
3. Place two pieces of the pastry inside the fryer and cook for 7 minutes
4. Remove and flatten a little, creating a hole in the middle
5. Add 1 tbsp of grated cheese to the hole you have created
6. Top the cheese with 1 tbsp of the ham
7. Crack one egg on top of the ham
8. Place back into the fryer and cook for 6 minutes
9. Repeat the same steps with the rest of the pastry

Chorizo & Potato Breakfast Pie

SERVINGS – 2

CALORIES – 401, PROTEIN – 21G, FAT – 26G, CARBS – 12G

Ingredients:

- 1 tbsp olive oil
- 1 chorizo sausage, sliced
- 1 boiled potato, cut into cubes
- 3 medium
- 1 can of sweetcorn, drained
- 50g/0.5 cups of feta cheese

Method:

1. Coat the frying basket with the olive oil
2. Place the chorizo, potato, and sweetcorn inside the fryer
3. Cook at 180C/350F, until the sausage has browned
4. Meanwhile, beat the eggs and pour over the sausage
5. Add the feta and cook for 5 minutes
6. Cool and cut into slices

Ham Breakfast Cups

SERVINGS – 4

CALORIES – 80, PROTEIN – 7G, FAT – 4G, CARBS – 11G

Ingredients:

- 2 slices of deli ham
- 4 medium eggs
- 8 slices of sandwich bread, toasted
- Salt and pepper for seasoning
- 4 ramekin dishes, greased with a little butter

Method:

1. Take a rolling pin and roll out the toast
2. Place two slices of toast inside each greased ramekin dish
3. Add a slice of ham around the sides of each ramekin
4. Crack one egg into each dish and season a little
5. Place in the air fryer and cook at 160C/320F for 15 minutes
6. Cool before serving

Crunchy Pepper & Onion Gratin

SERVINGS – 4

CALORIES – 294, PROTEIN – 5G, FAT – 6G, CARBS – 40G

Ingredients:

- 2 tbsp olive oil
- 1 green pepper, chopped
- 1 red pepper, chopped
- 1 onion, grated
- 4 large potatoes
- 1 tbsp black pepper
- 1 tsp cayenne pepper
- 1 tbsp salt
- 2 tbsp bicarbonate of soda

Method:

1. Take a large mixing bowl and place the grated potatoes inside
2. Add the bicarbonate of soda to the bowl and stir well. Set aside for 25 minutes
3. After 25 minutes has passed, drain the bowl and pat the potatoes dry
4. Take a large bowl and add the potatoes, black pepper, salt, cayenne pepper and olive oil, combine well
5. Transfer the mixture to your air fryer
6. Cook at 200C/390F for 10 minutes
7. Shake the potatoes and add the green peppers, red peppers, and the onion
8. Cook for a further 10 minutes

Simple Air Fryer Cheese Omelette

SERVINGS - 1

CALORIES - 200, PROTEIN - 11G, FAT - 3G, CARBS - 12G

Ingredients:

- 2 medium eggs
- 50ml/0.2 cups of milk
- 60g/0.5 cups of grated cheddar cheese
- Salt and pepper for seasoning

Method:

1. Crack the eggs into a large bowl and whisk with the milk
2. Season with salt and pepper and combine once more
3. Take a 6 x 3" baking pan and transfer the mixture to the pan
4. Place the pan into the fryer and cook for 170C/330F for 10 minutes
5. After 5 minutes have passed, use a spatula to loosen the edges and sprinkle the cheese on top
6. Cook for another 2 minutes

Egg Stuffed Peppers

SERVINGS - 2

CALORIES - 100, PROTEIN - 10G, FAT - 9G, CARBS - 5G

Ingredients:

- 1 tsp olive oil
- 1 bell pepper, halved
- 2 large eggs
- Salt and pepper for seasoning

Method:

1. Lightly grease the edges of the peppers with olive oil
2. Crack an egg into each half of the peppers and season
3. Place the peppers into your fryer - you may need to use a trivet so they don't fall over
4. Cook at 200C/390F for 13 minutes
5. Season again if required before serving

Cheese & Sausage Rolls

SERVINGS - 8

CALORIES - 504, PROTEIN - 4.1G, FAT - 2G, CARBS - 4G

Ingredients:

- 1 can of pizza dough
- 8 sausages, chopped
- 2 slices of cheese, quartered

Method:

1. Roll out the pizza dough and cut into four pieces
2. Add some of the sausage and cheese to the widest section
3. Roll the pizza dough up and tuck underneath to create a triangle shape
4. Repeat the same steps with all four pieces of dough
5. Place in the air fryer and cook at 190C/370F for 3 minutes

Bacon & Cheese Toast

SERVINGS - 2

CALORIES - 406, PROTEIN - 22G, FAT - 29G, CARBS - 27G

Ingredients:

- tbsp butter, melted
- 4 slices of regular sandwich bread
- 5 slices of bacon, cooked
- 2 slices of cheddar cheese
- 2 slices of cheddar cheese
- 2 slices of mozzarella cheese

Method:

1. Butter all slices of bread on one side
2. Place one slice of bread into the fryer, with the butter side down
3. Add the cheddar, bacon, and then the mozzarella on top
4. Place another slice of bread over the mozzarella, with the buttered side facing up
5. Cook at 170C/330F for 4 minutes
6. Turn over and cook for another 3 minutes
7. Repeat with the remaining bread

Ham Breakfast Sandwich

SERVINGS - 1
CALORIES - 294, PROTEIN - 2G, FAT - 3G, CARBS - 28G

Ingredients:

- 2 slices of regular sandwich bread
- 1 medium egg
- 4 slices of deli ham
- 4 slices of turkey
- 2 slices of Swiss cheese
- 0.25 tsp vanilla extract
- 1 tsp butter, melted

Method:

1. Combine the egg and vanilla extract in a small bowl
2. Place a slice of cheese, a slice of ham, and a slice of turkey between two slices of bread
3. Brush the butter over both sides of the sandwich
4. Dip the sandwich in the egg and let it rest for a minute
5. Place the sandwich in the fryer and cook at 200C/390F for 10 minutes
6. Turn over and cook for another 8 minutes

Homemade Jam Doughnuts, Breakfast-Style

SERVINGS - 4

CALORIES - 590, PROTEIN - 3G, FAT - 5G, CARBS - 30G

Ingredients:

- 1 packet of pizza dough
- 5 tbsp sugar
- 1 tbsp butter, melted
- 5 tbsp jam, raspberry or strawberry works well

Method:

1. Preheat the air fryer to 250C/480F
2. Arrange the pizza dough in the fryer basket and cook for 5 minutes
3. Place to one side once cooked
4. Take a mixing bowl and add the sugar
5. Dip each piece of the dough in the melted butter and then the sugar
6. Roll the dough carefully and add a little jam in the middle
7. Enjoy while still warm

Spinach, Eggs & Ham

SERVINGS - 4

CALORIES - 182, PROTEIN - 9G, FAT - 4G, CARBS - 22G

Ingredients:

- 1 tbsp olive oil
- 1 tbsp butter
- 4 tsp milk
- 4 medium eggs
- 200g/1.5 cups of deli ham
- 500g/4 cups of fresh spinach, wilted
- Salt and pepper to taste
- 4 ramekin dishes, greased with butter

Method:

1. Place the spinach, ham, 1 egg and a teaspoon of milk into each ramekin dish
2. Season to your liking
3. Arrange in the fryer basket and cook for 20 minutes

Sausage & Cheese Puffs

SERVINGS – 2

CALORIES – 204, PROTEIN – 2G, FAT – 3G, CARBS – 31G

Ingredients:

- 1 packet of puff pastry, defrosted
- 5 medium eggs
- 4 cooked sausages, broken up into pieces
- 50g/0.5 cups of cheddar cheese, grated
- 50g/0.5 cups of bacon, cooked

Method:

1. Take a medium frying pan and add the eggs, scrambling to your liking
2. Halfway through cooking the eggs, add the bacon and sausage, and stir well
3. Take the puff pastry and cut into rectangles
4. Once the egg is cooked, add a little of the mixture to each piece of pastry
5. Fold the pastry over and use a fork to seal the edges
6. Place into the air fryer basket and cook for 10 minutes at 190C/370F

Smashed, Spiced Eggs

SERVINGS – 2

CALORIES – 110, PROTEIN – 5G, FAT – 2G, CARBS – 12G

Ingredients:

- 4 medium eggs
- 1 tsp cayenne pepper
- Salt and pepper for seasoning
- Wire rack for cooking (air fryer safe)

Method:

1. Preheat your air fryer to 220C/420F
2. Place the wire rack into the air fryer and place the eggs on top
3. Cook your eggs for 15 minutes
4. Once cooked, remove and place in a bowl of ice cold water, resting for 5 minutes
5. Peel the eggs and use a fork to break them down a little
6. Season with cayenne pepper, salt and pepper before serving

Sweet Potato & Paprika Hash

SERVINGS – 6

CALORIES – 161, PROTEIN – 3G, FAT – 5G, CARBS – 30G

Ingredients:

- 2 tbsp olive oil
- 2 slices of bacon, chopped
- 2 sweet potatoes, cubed
- 1 tbsp smoked paprika
- Salt and pepper for seasoning

Method:

1. Preheat the air fryer to 200C/390F
2. Take a large bowl and add the oil, bacon, potatoes, and seasoning, combining well
3. Place into the air fryer and cook for 15 minutes
4. After 10 minutes, give everything a stir to loosen the edges

Breakfast Egg "Sandwich"

SERVINGS – 2

CALORIES – 303, PROTEIN – 3G, FAT – 3G, CARBS – 30G

Ingredients:

- Olive oil cooking spray
- 2 slices of regular sandwich bread
- 2 medium eggs
- Salt and pepper for seasoning

Method:

1. Preheat the air fryer to 190C/370F and spray with a little olive oil spray
2. Cut a hole into the middle of each slice of bread and place in the air fryer basket
3. Crack an egg into the hole and season
4. Cook for 5 minutes
5. Turn over and cook for another 2 minutes
6. Repeat the process with the other slice of bread

Cream Cheese & Jam Pockets

SERVINGS – 1

CALORIES – 205, PROTEIN – 3G, FAT – 5G, CARBS – 30G

Ingredients:

- 1 tbsp milk
- 1 medium egg
- 2 slices of regular sandwich bread
- 1 tbsp cream cheese
- 1 tbsp strawberry or raspberry jam

Method:

1. Spread the jam on one slice of bread
2. Take the other slice of bread and add the cream cheese to the middle of that slice
3. Use a butter knife to spread both the jam and cream cheese
4. Place the bread slices together, with the mixture in the middle
5. Combine the milk and eggs in a bowl
6. Preheat your fryer to 190C/370F and spray with a little oil beforehand
7. Dip the sandwich into the egg and make sure it's well coated
8. Place in the air fryer and cook for 5 minutes
9. Turn over and cook for another 2 minutes

AIR FRYER LUNCH RECIPES

At lunch time you might be in a rush. Busy work days, looking after the kids, appointments to get to, the list goes on. So, you want to make a delicious lunch that is low on health impact and high on flavour. It's time to grab your air fryer and create these mouthwatering lunch recipes!

Peppery Chicken Wings

SERVINGS - 2

CALORIES - 346, PROTEIN - 7G, FAT - 5G, CARBS - 30G

Ingredients:

- 1kg/2.2lb chicken wings
- 3 tbsp butter, melted
- 1 tsp honey
- ¼ tsp cayenne pepper
- 2 tsp lemon pepper seasoning, plus an extra 1tsp for the space

Method:

1. Preheat the air fryer to 260C/550F
2. Combine the lemon pepper seasoning and cayenne pepper in a bowl
3. Cover the chicken in the seasoning, ensuring everything is evenly coated
4. Arrange the chicken in the air fryer
5. Cook for 20 minutes, turning over at the halfway point
6. Turn the temperature up to 300C/570F and cook for another 6 minutes
7. Combine the melted butter with the honey and the rest of the seasoning mixture
8. Once the chicken wings have cooked, removed them from the air fryer basket
9. Pour the sauce over the top of the wings while they're still hot

Mediterranean Chicken Balls

SERVINGS - 4

CALORIES - 336, PROTEIN - 18G, FAT - 6G, CARBS - 31G

Ingredients:

- 500g/17oz ground chicken
- 1 large egg
- 1.5 tbsp garlic paste
- 1 tbsp dried oregano
- 1 tsp dried onion powder
- 1 tsp lemon zest
- Salt and pepper for seasoning

Method:

1. Preheat your air fryer to 260C/500F
2. Combine all ingredients into a large bowl, making sure everything is totally mixed together
3. Create meatballs using your hands. With this mixture, you should be able to create 12 evenly sized balls
4. Place the meatballs inside the air fryer, making sure there is some space between them
5. Cook for 9 minutes

Breaded Chicken Tenders

SERVINGS - 4

CALORIES - 213, PROTEIN - 26G, FAT - 11G, CARBS - 9G

Ingredients:

- 2 tbsp olive oil
- 8 frozen chicken tenders
- 1 egg, beaten
- 150g/5oz dried breadcrumbs

Method:

1. Preheat the air fryer to 175C/340F
2. Take a large bowl and combine the breadcrumbs and oil
3. Take one tender and it into the beaten egg, and then dip into the breadcrumb mixture, making sure it is fully coated
4. Carefully arrange the tender in the fryer basket
5. Repeat with the rest of the tenders
6. When placing them inside the air fryer, make sure they don't touch, and keep them on one even layer
7. Cook for 12 minutes
8. Check the chicken is cooked through before serving

Popcorn Shrimp With a Kick

SERVINGS - 2

CALORIES - 300, PROTEIN - 12G, FAT - 18G, CARBS - 11G

Ingredients:

- 300g/10oz popcorn shrimps, frozen
- 1 tsp cayenne pepper
- Salt and pepper for seasoning

Method:

1. Preheat the air fryer to 220C/420F
2. Place the shrimp inside the air fryer in an even layer
3. Cook for 6 minutes. At 3 minutes, shake the shrimp well and continue to cook until the full 6 minutes
4. Remove the shrimp when crispy
5. Before serving, season with the cayenne pepper, salt and pepper, to your liking

Panky   Calamari

SERVINGS - 2

CALORIES - 406, PROTEIN - 20G, FAT - 20G, CARBS - 21G

Ingredients:

- 250g/8.5oz plain flour
- 200ml/0.8 cups of buttermilk
- 1 egg
- 500g/17oz squid rings
- 500g/17oz panko breadcrumbs
- 2 tbsp pepper
- 2 tbsp salt

Method:

1. Preheat the air fryer at 150C/300F
2. Combine the buttermilk and egg in a large bowl and make sure everything is fully combined
3. Combine the salt, pepper, flour, and panko breadcrumbs in another bowl, making sure everything is mixed together
4. Dip the squid into the buttermilk, followed by the breadcrumbs. Make sure the squid is fully coated on all sides
5. Place in the air fryer basket, making sure they're arranged in an even layer and aren't touching
6. Cook for 12 minutes, until golden brown

Steak Bites

SERVINGS - 4

CALORIES - 316, PROTEIN - 31G, FAT - 51G, CARBS - 27G

Ingredients:

- 500g/17oz steak, cut into cubes
- 500g/17oz potato chips
- 2 eggs, beaten
- 100g/3.5oz flour
- Salt and pepper for seasoning

Method:

1. Preheat your air fryer to 260C/500F
2. Arrange the chips into your food processor and process unit you get fine crumbs
3. Combine the flour with salt and pepper in a large bowl
4. In another bowl, add the chips crumbs
5. Add the beaten egg to another bowl
6. Take the steak cubes and dip first in the flour, the egg, and the chip crumbs, making sure everything is fully coated on all sides
7. Arrange the steak bites into the air fryer and cook for 9 minutes

Beef & Courgette (Zucchini) Frittata

SERVINGS - 2

CALORIES - 214, PROTEIN - 13G, FAT - 31G, CARBS - 20G

Ingredients:

- 250g/8.8oz ground beef
- 250g/8.8oz grated cheese
- 4 hash browns, shredded
- 8 eggs

- Half an onion, diced
- 1 courgette/zucchini, diced
- Salt and pepper for seasoning

Method:

1. Preheat the air fryer to 260C/500F
2. Crumble the ground beef and place it in the air fryer basket
3. Add the onion and combine well
4. Cook for 3 minutes
5. Stir the mixture and cook for another 2 minutes
6. Remove the mixture and give the tray a clean
7. Add the courgette/zucchini to the air fryer
8. Cook for 3 minutes, stirring occasionally to make sure it doesn't stick
9. Add to the meat mixture and combine well
10. Combine the cheese, hash browns, and eggs in a large mixing bowl
11. Add the meat and courgette/zucchini to the bowl and season with a little salt and pepper
12. Transfer the mixture to a baking tray that will fit into your air fryer
13. Cook for 8 minutes
14. Cut lines in the top and continue to cook for a further 8 minutes
15. Allow to cool before cutting into slices

Swiss Cheese & Ham Sliders

SERVINGS – 4

CALORIES – 438, PROTEIN – 21G, FAT – 31G, CARBS – 4G

Ingredients:

- 600g/21oz minced lamb
- 2 tbsp Moroccan spice
- 2 tsp garlic puree
- 1 tsp harissa paste
- Salt and pepper for seasoning

Method:

1. Preheat the air fryer to 180C/350F
2. Take a large bowl and place all ingredients inside
3. Combine well to achieve a smooth mixture
4. Use your hands to create evenly sized patties
5. Place in the air fryer, making sure the patties don't touch and are on one even layer
6. Cook for 8 minutes

Potato & Carrot Burgers

SERVINGS – 4

CALORIES – 411, PROTEIN – 31G, FAT – 39G, CARBS – 22G

Ingredients:

- 8 slider bread rolls, halved
- 16 slices of Swiss cheese
- 16 slices of ham
- 5 tbsp mayonnaise
- 1 tsp onion powder
- ½ tsp paprika
- 1 tsp dill

Method:

1. Preheat your air fryer to 220C/420F
2. Take your halved slider rolls and place 2 slices of ham on each
3. Top with 2 slices of the Swiss cheese
4. Combine the mayonnaise with the onion powder, dill, and paprika in a large mixing bowl
5. Add half a tablespoon of the sauce on top of each piece of cheese
6. Place the top on the bread slider to create a sandwich
7. Carefully place the sandwich inside the air fryer basket
8. Cook for 5 minutes before turning over and cooking for another 5 minutes

Italian Ravioli

SERVINGS - 12

CALORIES - 206, PROTEIN - 21G, FAT - 20G, CARBS - 23G

Ingredients:

- 1 tbsp oil
- 100ml hot water
- 150g/5oz instant mashed potato
- 50g/1.7oz frozen peas and carrots, defrosted
- 2 tbsp coriander
- ½ tsp turmeric
- ½ tsp cumin seeds
- ¼ tsp ground cumin
- ½ tsp cayenne
- ½ tsp salt

Method:

1. Spray the inside of the air fryer with a little cooking spread and preheat to 200C/390F
2. Take a large bowl and add all the ingredients inside
3. Combine everything together well and place to one side to rest for 10 minutes
4. Use your hands to create 12 evenly sized patties
5. Arrange the patties inside the air fryer, ensuring they don't touch and they're all on an even layer
6. Cook for 10 minutes

Onion Dumplings

SERVINGS - 2

CALORIES - 309, PROTEIN - 2G, FAT - 8G, CARBS - 11G

Ingredients:

- 1 tbsp olive oil
- 14 pierogi dumplings, frozen
- 1 onion, sliced
- 1 tsp sugar

Method:

1. Fill a large saucepan with water and bring to the boil
2. Cook the dumplings for 5 minutes
3. Once cooked, removed and drain carefully
4. Add a small amount of oil to the air fryer basket and preheat to 220C/428F
5. Cook the onion for 12 minutes, giving it a stir every so often
6. After 5 minutes, add the sugar to the air fryer and combine well
7. Remove the onions from the air fryer and set aside
8. Add the cooked dumplings to the air fryer and cook for 4 minutes
9. Increase the temperature up to 270C/518F and cook for 3 minutes extra
10. Combine the dumplings with the onions and serve

Italian Aubergine (Eggplant) Parmesan

SERVINGS - 2

CALORIES - 246, PROTEIN - 21G, FAT - 25G, CARBS - 23G

Ingredients:

- 1 egg
- 1 tbsp water
- 1 large aubergine/eggplant, sliced
- 4 slices of wholewheat bread - create breadcrumbs out of these
- 3 tbsp Parmesan cheese, grated

- 30g/1oz mozzarella cheese, grated
- 1 tsp Italian seasoning
- 3 tbsp whole wheat flour
- 5 tbsp marinara sauce
- Salt for seasoning

Method:

1. Take the aubergine/eggplant and season both sides. Set to one side for 30 minutes
2. Preheat the air fryer to 270C/518F
3. Combine the egg, flour, and water in a bowl and make sure everything is mixed together well
4. Take a plate and add the breadcrumbs, parmesan, and Italian seasoning, combining well to create a coating
5. Dip the aubergine/eggplant into the egg mixture and then the breadcrumbs, making sure it is fully coated on all sides
6. Carefully arrange the aubergine/eggplant into the air fryer basket and cook for 8 minutes
7. Add the marinara sauce and mozzarella on top and cook for another 2 minutes

Spicy Buffalo Wings

SERVINGS - 4

CALORIES - 228, FAT - 41G, PROTEIN - 20G, CARBS - 7G

Ingredients:

- 500g/17oz chicken wings
- 2 tbsp vinegar
- 1 tbsp olive oil
- 75g/2.6oz butter
- 5 tbsp cayenne pepper sauce
- ¼ tsp cayenne pepper
- 1 tsp garlic powder

Method:

1. Preheat your air fryer to 182C/350F
2. Place the chicken wings into a large bowl
3. Drizzle oil over the wings, tossing to coat evenly
4. Place the wings inside the air fryer basket and cook for 25 minutes
5. Turn the wings and cook for another 5 minutes
6. Take a saucepan and heat over a medium temperature on your hob
7. Add the hot pepper sauce, butter, vinegar, garlic powder, and cayenne pepper, mixing together well
8. Pour the sauce over the wings and flip to coat, before serving

Zingy Salmon Burgers

SERVINGS - 7

CALORIES - 503, FAT - 22G, PROTEIN - 14G, CARBS - 22G

Ingredients:

- 2 medium eggs
- 1 can of salmon, drained
- 30g panko breadcrumbs
- Zest of 1 lime
- 1.5 tbsp brown sugar
- 1.5 tbsp Thai red curry paste
- Salt and pepper for seasoning

Method:

1. Preheat the air fryer to 180C/350F
2. Combine all ingredients in a large bowl
3. Create patties with your hands – you're aiming for around 1" thick patties
4. Place the patties into the air fryer
5. Cook for 4 minutes
6. Turn over and cook for another 4 minutes

Fishy Sticks

SERVINGS - 2

CALORIES - 205, FAT - 46G, PROTEIN - 11G, CARBS - 6G

Ingredients:

- 1 fillet of white fish - your choice
- 50g/0.5 cups of flour
- 2 slices of whole meal bread, grated
- 1 egg,
- Juice of 1 lemon

- 1 tsp mixed herbs
- 1 tsp parsley
- 1 tsp thyme
- Salt and pepper for seasoning

Method:

1. Preheat your air fryer to 180C/350F
2. Combine the breadcrumbs in a bowl with the parsley and seasoning
3. Crack the egg into a separate bowl and whisk
4. Take another bowl and add the flour
5. Combine the fish, thyme, lemon juice, pepper, salt, and mixed herbs in a bender, creating a breadcrumb-like consistency
6. Create stick shapes out of the fish mixture
7. Dip the sticks into the flour first, then the egg, and finally the breadcrumbs
8. Place in the air fryer and cook for 8 minutes at 180C/350F

Spicy Salmon Burgers

SERVINGS - 4

CALORIES - 200, PROTEIN - 22G, FAT - 11G, CARBS - 23G

Ingredients:

- 1 egg
- 1 onion, diced
- 1 tsp dill weed
- 400g/14oz salmon
- 200g/1.5 cups of breadcrumbs

Method:

1. Take a large bowl and add the egg, onion, dill weed and breadcrumbs, combining well
2. Add the salmon and break into pieces, incorporating it into the mixture
3. Use your hands to create patties with the mixture
4. Place the patties in the air fryer
5. Cook for 5 minutes at 180C/350F
6. Turn over and cook for another 5 minutes

Tomato Ravioli

SERVINGS - 4

CALORIES - 257, PROTEIN - 11G, FAT - 14G, CARBS - 30G

Ingredients:

- 1 tbsp olive oil
- 200g/1.5 cups of breadcrumbs
- 200ml/0.8 cups of buttermilk
- 1 pack of frozen ravioli
- 5 tbsp marinara sauce

Method:

1. Preheat your air fryer to 220C/420F
2. Place the breadcrumbs in one mixing bowl, and the buttermilk in another bowl
3. Take your ravioli and dip first in the buttermilk and then into the breadcrumbs
4. Place into the air fryer and cook for 7 minutes
5. Serve with the sauce over the top

Cheesy Pasta Quiche

SERVINGS – 4

CALORIES – 181, PROTEIN – 9G, FAT – 7G, CARBS – 19G

Ingredients:

- 1 block of regular shortcrust pastry, defrosted
- 150ml/0.6 cups of milk
- 400g/3.2 cups of cheese, grated
- 8 tbsp pasta, macaroni works well here
- 2 medium eggs
- 2 tbsp Greek yogurt
- 1 tsp garlic puree
- 4 ramekin dishes, greased

Method:

1. Line the inside of each ramekin with the shortcrust pastry
2. Take a bowl and add the pasta, garlic puree, and yogurt, combining well
3. Place some of the mixture into each ramekin, to around 3/4 of the way up the dish
4. Take a small bowl and combine the milk and egg
5. Pour over the top of each dish and sprinkle with some of the cheese
6. Place in the air fryer and cook for 20 minutes at 180C/350F

Lentil & Mushroom Balls

SERVINGS – 4

CALORIES – 609, PROTEIN – 22G, FAT – 19G, CARBS – 91G

Ingredients:

- 400ml/1.6 cups of water
- 2 cans of lentils, drained
- 100g/0.8 cups of breadcrumbs
- 3 tbsp dried mushrooms
- 200g/1.5 cups of walnut halves
- 3 tbsp parsley
- 1.5 tbsp tomato paste
- Salt and pepper for seasoning

Method:

1. Preheat your air fryer to 190C/374F
2. Combine the dried mushrooms, lentils, parsley, walnuts, tomato paste and seasoning in a blender
3. Add the breadcrumbs and fold in
4. Use your hands to create balls out of the mixture
5. Place in the air fryer and cook for 10 minutes
6. Turn and cook for another 5 minutes

Cheesy Potato Slice

SERVINGS - 4

CALORIES - 202, PROTEIN - 7G, FAT - 11G, CARBS - 15G

Ingredients:

- 2 eggs, beaten
- 1 tbsp plain flour
- 50g/0.4 cups of cheddar cheese, grated
- 100ml/0.4 cups of coconut cream
- 2 large potatoes, sliced
- 4 ramekin dishes

Method:

1. Preheat the air fryer to 180C/350F
2. Place the potato slices into the air fryer and cook for 10 minutes
3. Take a bowl and add the flour, eggs, and coconut cream, combining well
4. Once the potato slices are cooked, line the inside of the ramekin dishes with the slices
5. Pour the mixture inside the ramekins and sprinkle the cheese over the top
6. Place in the air fryer and cook for 10 minutes at 200C/390F

Artichoke & Pumpkin Pasta

SERVINGS - 2

CALORIES - 406, PROTEIN - 11G, FAT - 23G, CARBS - 24G

Ingredients:

- 1 tsp olive oil
- 6 artichoke hearts
- 1 clove of garlic
- 1 can of chickpeas, drained
- 2 tbsp pumpkin seeds
- 100g/1 cup of pasta - your choice
- 50g0.5 cups of basil leaves, chopped
- 2 tbsp lemon juice
- ½ tsp white miso paste

Method:

1. Preheat the air fryer to 200C/392F
2. Cook the chickpeas in the air fryer basket for 12 minutes
3. Meanwhile, cook the pasta to your liking
4. Add the rest of the ingredients inside your food processor and blend well
5. Transfer the cooked pasta to a serving bowl and pour the mixture over the top, combining well
6. Sprinkle the cooked chickpeas over the top before serving

Pepperoni & Basil Bagel

SERVINGS - 1

CALORIES - 393, PROTEIN - 12G, FAT - 4G, CARBS - 60G

Ingredients:

- 2 tbsp marinara sauce
- 1 bagel, halved
- 2 tbsp mozzarella cheese
- 6 slices pepperoni
- Pinch of basil to serve

Method:

1. Heat your air fryer to 180C/350F
2. Place the bagel halves into the air fryer and cook for 2 minutes
3. Once cooked, add marinara sauce, pepperoni and the mozzarella cheese on top
4. Cook for another 4 minutes
5. Add the basil on top before serving

Saucy Meatball Sub

SERVINGS - 2

CALORIES - 389, PROTEIN - 13G, FAT - 34G, CARBS - 31G

Ingredients:

- 2 hotdog or sub rolls
- 160g/1.2 cups of parmesan cheese, grated
- 8 pork meatballs - frozen work well here
- 5 tbsp marinara sauce
- ¼ tsp dried oregano

Method:

1. Preheat your air fryer to 220C/420F
2. Cook the frozen meatballs for 10 minutes, turning at the 5 minute mark
3. Once cooked, coat the meatballs in the marinara sauce and the oregano
4. Place the meatballs into the hotdog or sub roll, along with any extra sauce
5. Add the cheese and place back in the air fryer
6. Cook for 2 minutes

Steak Cheesy Chips

SERVINGS - 2

CALORIES - 556, PROTEIN - 31G, FAT - 30G, CARBS - 21G

Ingredients:

- 1 bag of frozen French fries/ chips
- 500g/14oz sirloin steak
- 2 tbsp steak seasoning
- 350g/3 cups of cheddar cheese, grated
- 2 tbsp guacamole
- 2 tbsp sour cream
- Salt and pepper to taste

Method:

1. Preheat the air fryer to 260C/500F
2. Season the steak and add to the air fryer, cooking for 4 minutes
3. Turn over and cook for another 4 minutes
4. Set aside once cooked
5. Place the frozen fries/chips inside the air fryer and cook for 5 minutes, giving them a shake at the halfway point
6. Add the cheese on top of the fries/chips and continue cooking for another 2 minutes
7. Cut the steak into chunks and place on top of the melted cheese
8. Cook for another 30 seconds

Cheesy Garlic Burgers

SERVINGS - 4

CALORIES - 384, PROTEIN - 21G, FAT - 22G, CARBS - 42G

Ingredients:

- 400g/14oz minced beef
- 1 onion, chopped
- 2 tbsp Worcestershire sauce
- 250g/2 cups of feta cheese, crumbled
- 25g/0.2 cups of green olive, chopped
- 0.5 tsp steak seasoning
- 0.5 tsp garlic powder
- Salt and pepper for seasoning

Method:

1. Place all the ingredients into a large mixing bowl and combine well
2. Use your hands to create four large patties
3. Place the patties in the air fryer
4. Cook for 15 minutes at 200C/390F

Stuffed Peppers With Lamb

SERVINGS – 4

CALORIES – 372, PROTEIN – 41G, FAT – 15G, CARBS – 33G

Ingredients:

- 75g/0.5 cups of rice, cooked
- 500g/1lb minced lamb
- 2 tsp Worcestershire sauce
- 4 bell peppers, tops cut off and deseeded
- 1 onion, chopped
- 1 garlic clove, minced

- 5 tbsp tomato sauce
- 100g/0.8 cups of cheese, grated
- 0.5 tsp chilli powder
- 1 tsp garlic powder
- 1 tsp dried basil
- Salt and pepper for seasoning

Method:

1. Preheat the air fryer to 200C/390F
2. Add the minced lamb, onions, seasonings and garlic and cook until the minced lamb is brown
3. Remove from the heat and add the rice, half the cheese, Worcestershire sauce, and most of the tomato sauce, combining well
4. Place the mixture inside the peppers and arrange inside the air fryer
5. Cook for 11 minutes – in the last couple of minutes, add the rest of the tomato sauce and the cheese over the top of the peppers

Lamb & Jalapeño Empanadas

SERVINGS - 12

CALORIES - 436, PROTEIN - 13G, FAT - 17G, CARBS - 23G

Ingredients:

- 2 tsp olive oil
- 2 packs of shortcrust pastry, defrosted
- 1 egg
- 50g/0.4 cups of cheddar cheese, grated
- 50g/0.4 cups of pepper jack cheese
- 500g/4 cups of minced lamb
- 1 onion, chopped
- 1 clove of garlic, chopped
- 2 tbsp jalapeño, chopped
- Salt and pepper for seasoning

Method:

1. Heat the oil in a medium frying pan and cook the garlic and onion until softened
2. Add the minced lamb, jalapeños, garlic, and a little seasoning. Cook until the meat has browned
3. Set the pan aside to cool
4. Roll out the pastry thinly and use a cutter to create circles
5. Add 1 tablespoon of the meat mixture and a little cheese
6. Fold the pastry over and use a fork to seal the edges
7. Beat the egg and brush over the pastry
8. Place in the air fryer and cook for 12 minutes at 170C/330F

Pork & Bacon Roulade

SERVINGS - 2

CALORIES - 413, PROTEIN - 22G, FAT - 30G, CARBS - 9G

Ingredients:

- 2 tbsp olive oil
- 400g/14oz pork steak
- 4 strips of bacon, chopped
- 1 onion, sliced
- 1 tbsp tomato paste

- 4 tbsp sour cream
- 1 tsp chopped parsley
- 2 tbsp Dijon mustard
- Salt and pepper for seasoning

Method:

1. Season the onions and place in the air fryer
2. Cook at 200C/390F for 6 minutes
3. Transfer the cooked onions to a bowl and add the parsley, tomato paste and sour cream, combining well
4. Take the pork steak and spread the Dijon mustard over the top
5. Add the bacon and onion
6. Roll up the steak and place in the air fryer, cooking for 10 minutes, or until completely cooked through

Cayenne Wings

SERVINGS - 2

CALORIES - 396, PROTEIN - 3G, FAT - 4G, CARBS - 32G

Ingredients:

- 1kg/2.2lb chicken wings
- 3 tbsp butter, melted
- ¼ tsp cayenne pepper
- 1 tsp honey
- 2 tsp lemon pepper seasoning

Method:

1. Preheat your air fryer to 260C/550F
2. Take a bowl and combine the cayenne pepper and the lemon pepper
3. Coat the chicken with the mixture and place in the air fryer
4. Cook for 20 minutes, turning after 10 minutes have passed
5. Increase the temperature to 300C/570F and cook for another 7 minutes
6. Take a bowl and combine the honey and butter
7. Remove the wings and pour the mixture over the top

Spicy Meatloaf

SERVINGS - 4

CALORIES - 270, PROTEIN - 21G, FAT - 12G, CARBS - 5G

Ingredients:

- 500g/1lb minced lamb
- 1 onion, diced
- 2 eggs
- 200g/1.5 cups coriander/ cilantro, sliced
- 1 tbsp minced ginger
- 1 tbsp minced garlic
- A quarter of a cardamom pod
- 1 tsp cayenne pepper
- 2 tsp garam masala
- 1 tsp salt
- 1 tsp turmeric
- 0.5 tsp cinnamon

Method:

1. Take a large bowl and add all ingredients
2. Combine together until you have a smooth consistency
3. Take an 8" cooking pan and place inside the air fryer
4. Set the air fryer to 180C/350F
5. Cook for 15 minutes
6. Allow to cool slightly before slicing

Garlic Chicken Chunks

SERVINGS - 4

CALORIES - 366, PROTEIN - 11G, FAT - 7G, CARBS - 38G

Ingredients:

- 500g/1lb ground chicken
- 1.5 tbsp garlic paste
- 1 large egg
- 1 tsp lemon zest
- 1 tbsp dried oregano
- 1 tsp dried onion powder
- Salt and pepper for seasoning

Method:

1. Preheat the air fryer to 260C/500F
2. Take a large bowl and combine all ingredients, creating a smooth mixture
3. Use your hands to create balls, making sure they are all even
4. Place inside the fryer and cook for 9 minutes

Spicy Potato Balls

SERVINGS - 12

CALORIES - 222, PROTEIN - 24G, FAT - 25G, CARBS - 23G

Ingredients:

- 1 tbsp oil
- 150g/1.2 cups of mashed potato
- 50g/0.4 cups of peas and carrots mixture, defrosted
- 2 tbsp coriander
- 0.5 tsp cumin seeds
- 0.5 tsp turmeric
- 0.5 tsp cayenne pepper
- 0.25 tsp ground cumin
- Salt and pepper for seasoning
- 100ml hot water

Method:

1. Preheat the air fryer to 200C/390F
2. Place all ingredients inside a large bowl and combine well
3. Leave to rest for 15 minutes
4. Use your hands to create patties out of the mixture, making sure they're evenly sized
5. Place inside the air fryer and cook for 10 minutes

AIR FRYER DINNER RECIPES

After a busy day at work, the last thing you want to do is start grabbing multiple pans and cooking full meals. Your air fryer has you covered. You can easily make a truly sumptuous meal with your appliance, with less stress and a lot of flavour. When you add meal planning into the equation, everything becomes even easier!

Which of these fantastic air fryer dinner recipes will you try first?

Mushroom & Turkey Cutlets

SERVINGS - 2

CALORIES - 406, PROTEIN - 26G, FAT - 20G, CARBS - 17G

Ingredients:

- 160ml/0.6 cups of milk
- 2 turkey cutlets
- 1 tbsp butter, melted
- 1 can of cream of mushroom sauce
- Salt and pepper for seasoning

Method:

1. Preheat the air fryer to 220C/428F
2. Brush the turkey cults with the butter and add a little seasoning
3. Place in the air fryer, leaving a little space between them and cook for 11 minutes
4. Take a saucepan and add the mushroom soup and milk
5. Cook over a medium heat for around 10 minutes, stirring occasionally
6. Pour the sauce over the turkey cutlets before serving

Spicy Chicken Chimichangas

SERVINGS - 6

CALORIES - 406, PROTEIN - 21G, FAT - 22G, CARBS - 26G

Ingredients:

- 100g/3.5oz shredded cooked chicken
- 6 flour tortillas
- 150g/5oz nacho cheese
- 1 jalapeño pepper, chopped
- 60g/2oz refried beans

- 5 tbsp salsa
- 0.5 tsp chill powder
- 1 tsp cumin
- Salt and pepper for seasoning

Method:

1. Spray the air fryer with a little cooking spray and preheat to 200C/390F
2. Add all of the ingredients into a large bowl and combine well
3. Take your tortillas and add ⅓ of the filling to each
4. Roll the tortillas into a burrito shape
5. Place the tortillas in the air fryer in one even layer
6. Cook for 7 minutes

Furikake & Mayo Salmon

Ingredients:

- 1 salmon fillet
- 150ml/0.6 cups of mayonnaise
- 2 tbsp furikake
- 1 tbsp soy sauce
- Salt and pepper for seasoning

Method:

1. Preheat your air fryer to 230C/446F
2. Combine the mayonnaise and soy sauce in a small bowl
3. Season the salmon on both sides
4. Place the salmon into the air fryer with the skin side down
5. Brush the mayonnaise mixture on top of the salmon evenly
6. Sprinkle the furikake on top of the salmon
7. Cook for 10 minutes

Breaded Fish Fillets With Ranch

Ingredients:

- 4 fish fillets - your choice
- 2 tbsp oil
- 200g/7oz breadcrumbs
- 30g/1oz ranch-style dressing mix
- 2 eggs, beaten
- Lemon wedges to garnish

Method:

1. Preheat your air fryer to 180C/356F
2. Take a bowl and combine the breadcrumbs and ranch dressing
3. Add the oil until the mix becomes smooth
4. Dip the fish into the breadcrumb mixture, making sure it is covered evenly on all sides
5. Carefully place the fish into the air fryer and cook for 13 minutes

Traditional Beef Wellington

SERVINGS – 4

CALORIES – 202, PROTEIN – 31G, FAT – 21G, CARBS – 28G

Ingredients:

- 600g/21oz beef fillet
- 300g/10oz chicken liver pate
- 1 egg, beaten
- 500g/17oz shortcrust pastry
- Salt and pepper for seasoning

Method:

1. Season the beef with a little salt and pepper
2. Wrap the beef in cling film and place in the refrigerator for 1 hour
3. Meanwhile, take the shortcrust pastry and roll it out
4. Brush the edges of the pastry with beaten egg
5. Spread the pate over the pastry in an even layer
6. Take the beef out of the refrigerator and remove the clingfilm
7. Place the beef in the centre of the pastry and wrap it around, sealing around the meat 8. Preheat your air fryer to 160C/320F
8. Place the beef into the air fryer and cook for 35 minutes

Coconut & Ginger Beef

SERVINGS - 2

CALORIES - 336, PROTEIN - 12G, FAT - 31G, CARBS - 13G

Ingredients:

- 600g/21oz steak, sliced thinly
- 25ml/0.2 cups of water
- 100g/3.5oz brown sugar
- ½ tbsp minced garlic
- 1 tbsp coconut oil
- 2 red peppers, sliced

- 25g/0.8oz liquid aminos
- ¼ tsp pepper
- ½ tsp ground ginger
- 1 tsp red pepper flakes
- ¼ tsp salt

Method:

1. Take a saucepan and add the coconut oil, melting over a medium heat
2. Add the sliced red pepper and cook until soft
3. Take another pan to add the aminos, brown sugar, ginger, garlic, and pepper flakes, combining well
4. Bring the pan to the boil, then turn the temperature down and simmer for 10 mins
5. Preheat the air fryer to 200C/392F
6. Season the steak with salt and pepper
7. Place the steak inside the air fryer and cook for 10 minutes.
8. Turn the steak and cook for a further 5 minutes until crispy
9. Transfer the steak to the pepper mixture and combing with the ginger sauce

Classic Beef Satay

SERVINGS – 2

CALORIES – 446, PROTEIN – 21G, FAT – 16G, CARBS – 15G

Ingredients:

- 2 tbsp oil
- 400g/14oz steak, cut into strips
- 25g/0.8oz roasted peanuts
- 1 tbsp fish sauce
- 1 tsp sriracha sauce
- 1 tbsp soy sauce

- 1 tbsp sugar
- 200g/7oz fresh coriander, sliced
- 1 tsp ground coriander/cilantro
- 1 tbsp minced ginger
- 1 tbsp minced garlic

Method:

1. Take a large bowl and add the oil, fish sauce, soy, ginger, garlic, sugar sriracha, coriander, and ¼ cup coriander/cilantro. Combine well
2. Add the steak to the bowl, combine and marinate for 30 minutes
3. Preheat the air fryer to 200C/392F
4. Add the steak to the air fryer and cook for 8 minutes
5. Transfer the steak onto a plate and top with the remaining coriander/ cilantro and chopped peanuts

Mustard & Garlic Pork Tenderloin

SERVINGS - 2

CALORIES - 497, PROTEIN - 30G, FAT - 37G, CARBS - 22G

Ingredients:

- 3 tbsp olive oil
- 1 pork tenderloin
- 1 tbsp dijon mustard
- 3 tbsp soy sauce
- 2 minced garlic cloves
- 2 tbsp brown sugar
- Salt and pepper for seasoning

Method:

1. Take a large bowl and combine all the ingredients, except for the pork
2. Pour the mixture into a ziplock bag and then add the pork, sealing the bag
3. Place the bag into the refrigerator for 30 minutes
4. Preheat your air fryer to 260C/500F
5. Remove the pork from the bag and place it in the air fryer
6. Cook for 25 minutes, being sure to turn the pork over at the halfway point
7. Remove and rest for 5 minutes
8. Slice into pieces

Balsamic Pork Chops with Raspberry

SERVINGS - 4

CALORIES - 569, PROTEIN - 31G, FAT - 30G, CARBS - 32G

Ingredients:

- 2 eggs
- 4 pork chops
- 30ml/0.2 cups of milk
- 30ml/0.2 cups of balsamic vinegar
- 1 tbsp orange juice

- 250g/8.8oz panko breadcrumbs
- 250g/8.8oz pecans, finely chopped
- 2 tbsp brown sugar
- 2 tbsp raspberry jam

Method:

1. Preheat the air fryer to 200C/390F
2. Take a medium mixing bowl and combine the eggs and milk
3. Take a separate bowl and combine the breadcrumbs and pecans
4. Take the pork chops and coat in the flour, egg and then the breadcrumbs
5. Place in the air fryer and cook for 12 minutes until golden, being sure to turn at the halfway point
6. Take a pan and place the remaining ingredients inside
7. Simmer over a medium heat for around 6 minutes
8. Serve the sauce with the pork chops

Balsamic Gnocchi Caprese

SERVINGS - 2

CALORIES - 206, PROTEIN - 20G, FAT - 15G, CARBS - 20G

Ingredients:

- 2 tbsp olive oil
- 1 pack of gnocchi
- 150g/5oz cherry tomatoes, halved
- 150g/5oz Parmesan, grated
- 200g/7oz mini mozzarella balls

- 2 tbsp balsamic vinegar
- 3 cloves of garlic, pressed
- 200g/7oz basil, chopped
- Salt and pepper for seasoning

Method:

1. Preheat the air fryer to 220C/428F
2. Take a large bowl and add the gnocchi, cherry tomatoes, balsamic vinegar, oil, garlic, and seasoning. Combine everything well
3. Transfer the mixture to the air fryer basket
4. Cook for 10 minutes, shaking the basket every few minutes
5. Once cooked, transfer everything to a large mixing bowl
6. Add the Parmesan cheese and combine to coat
7. Add the mozzarella and basil, combining well before serving

Garlic & Citrus Cauliflower

SERVINGS – 2

CALORIES – 376, PROTEIN – 20G, FAT – 15G, CARBS – 12G

Ingredients:

- 2 tsp olive oil
- Head of cauliflower, cut into florets
- 200ml/0.8 cups of water
- 200g/7oz flour
- 2 garlic cloves, minced
- 1 tsp minced ginger
- 150ml/0.6 cups of orange juice
- 3 tbsp white vinegar

- 1/2 tsp red pepper flakes
- 1 tsp sesame oil
- 100g/3.5oz brown sugar
- 3 tbsp soy sauce
- 1 tbsp cornstarch
- 2 tbsp water
- 1 tsp salt

Method:

1. Preheat the air fryer to 220C/428F
2. Add the water, salt, and flour into a large mixing bowl and combine
3. Dip each floret of cauliflower into the mixture and place it in the air fryer basket afterwards
4. Cook for 15 minutes
5. Meanwhile, make the orange sauce. Add all the remaining ingredients into a pan and combine
6. Heat over a medium temperature and allow to simmer for 3 minutes. The sauce should thicken
7. Drizzle the sauce over the cauliflower before serving

Falafel Patties

SERVINGS - 2

CALORIES - 700, PROTEIN - 32G, FAT - 27G, CARBS - 90G

Ingredients:

- 1 can of chickpeas
- 4 tbsp soft cheese
- 1 onion
- The rind and juice of 1 lemon
- 140g/5oz oats
- 3 tbsp Greek yogurt
- 28g/0.9oz cheddar cheese, grated

- 28g/0.9oz feta cheese
- 1 tbsp garlic puree
- 1 tbsp coriander
- 1 tbsp oregano
- 1 tbsp parsley
- Salt and pepper to taste

Method:

1. Place the chickpeas, lemon rind, garlic, onion, and seasonings into a food processor and blitz until coarse
2. Preheat the air fryer to 180C/350F
3. Transfer the mix to a bowl and stir in half the soft cheese, feta, and cheddar cheese
4. Use your hands to form patties
5. Place the oats onto a plate and roll the patties on the plate to coat well
6. Place in the air fryer and cook for 8 minutes
7. Take a bowl and combine the remaining soft cheese, greek yogurt, and lemon juice to make the serving sauce

Tikka Paneer

SERVINGS - 2

CALORIES - 306, PROTEIN - 13G, FAT - 20G, CARBS - 21G

Ingredients:

- 1 tbsp olive oil
- 200ml/0.8 cups of yogurt
- 1 chopped onion
- 1 chopped green pepper
- 1 chopped red pepper
- 1 chopped yellow pepper
- 250g paneer cheese, cubed
- 1 tsp ginger garlic paste

- 1 tsp red chilli powder
- 1 tsp garam masala
- 1 tsp turmeric powder
- 1 tbsp dried fenugreek leaves
- The juice of 1 lemon
- 2 tbsp chopped coriander/cilantro
- 8 metal skewers

Method:

1. Combine the yogurt, garlic paste, red chilli powder, turmeric powder, garam masala, lemon juice, fenugreek, and chopped coriander/ cilantro in a bowl. Place to one side to rest for 10 minutes
2. Add the cheese and coat well
3. Leave to marinate for 2 hours in the refrigerator
4. Preheat your air fryer to 220C/428F
5. Take 8 metal skewers and thread the peppers, onions, and cheese alternately
6. Drizzle a little oil over the top of the skewers
7. Arrange in the air fryer and cook for 3 minutes
8. Turn over and cook for a further 3 minutes

Creamy Mushroom Pasta

SERVINGS - 4

CALORIES - 400, PROTEIN - 11G, FAT - 31G, CARBS - 9G

Ingredients:

- 250g/8.8oz mushrooms, sliced
- 300g/10oz cooked pasta - your choice
- 1 onion, chopped
- 75g/2.6oz double cream/heavy cream
- 30g/1oz parmesan, grated
- 70g/2.5oz mascarpone

- 2 tsp minced garlic
- ½ tsp red pepper flakes
- 1 tsp dried thyme
- 1 tsp ground black pepper
- 1 tsp salt

Method:

1. Take a bowl and combine all ingredients
2. Preheat the air fryer to 175C/347F
3. Grease a 7x3 inch pan and add the mixture inside
4. Place the pan into the air fryer and cook for 15 minutes
5. Halfway through, give the mixture a stir
6. Pour the sauce over the cooked pasta, stir and sprinkle with the parmesan

Garlic Buttermilk Chicken

SERVINGS – 4

CALORIES – 305, FAT – 41G, PROTEIN – 20G, CARBS – 7G

Ingredients:

- 500g/17oz chicken thighs, boneless
- 75g/2.6oz all-purpose flour
- ½ tsp brown sugar
- 180ml/0.7 cups of buttermilk
- 40g/1.4oz tapioca flour
- 1 egg, beaten
- ½ tsp garlic salt
- 1 tsp garlic powder
- ½ tsp paprika
- ½ tsp onion powder
- ¼ tsp oregano
- Salt and pepper for seasoning

Method:

1. Combine the buttermilk and hot sauce in a mixing bowl
2. Add the garlic salt, tapioca flour, and black pepper into a plastic bag and shake to combine
3. Take the chicken thighs and add to the buttermilk to coat
4. Coat in the tapioca mixture, the egg, and then the flour
5. Preheat the air fryer to 190C/374F
6. Cook the chicken thighs for 10 minutes
7. Make sure the chicken is white in the middle before serving

Cauliflower & Fish Bowls

SERVINGS - 2

CALORIES - 482, PROTEIN - 13G, FAT - 13G, CARBS - 11G

Ingredients:

- 400g/1lb fish - your choice
- 1 avocado, sliced
- 300g/2.5 cups of cauliflower rice
- 25g/0.2 cups of sour cream
- 25g/0.2 cups of pickled onions
- 0.5 tsp cumin

- 1 tsp chilli powder
- 0.5 tsp paprika
- 1 tbsp lime juice
- 1 tbsp sriracha
- 25g/0.2 cups of fresh coriander/cilantro
- Salt and pepper for seasoning

Method:

1. Preheat your air fryer to 200C/390F
2. Take a bowl and combine the cumin, paprika, chilli powder, salt and pepper
3. Cover both sides of the fish with the spice mixture
4. Place inside the air fryer and cook for 12 minutes
5. Meanwhile, cook the cauliflower rice to the instructions on the packet
6. Add the coriander/cilantro and lime juice once cooked, combining well
7. Combine the rice, avocado, fish and pickled onions in two separate serving bowls
8. Take a small bowl and combine the sriracha and sour cream
9. Pour the mixture over the top before serving

Salt & Pepper Scallops

SERVINGS - 2

CALORIES - 406, PROTEIN - 22G, FAT - 46G, CARBS - 33G

Ingredients:

- 1 tbsp olive oil
- 6 scallops
- Salt and pepper for seasoning

Method:

1. Coat the scallops with the oil and season with salt and pepper
2. Place in the air fryer
3. Cook for 2 minutes at 200C/390F
4. Turn over and cook for a further 2 minutes before serving

Mayonnaise Fish Fingers

SERVINGS - 4

CALORIES - 411, PROTEIN - 4G, FAT - 32G, CARBS - 30G

Ingredients:

- 400g/14oz cod fillets, cut into stick-shapes
- 300g/2.5 cups of panko breadcrumbs
- 2 tbsp dill pickle
- 6 tbsp mayonnaise
- 1 tsp seafood seasoning

Method:

1. Preheat the air fryer to 200C/390F
2. Take a large bowl and add the dill pickle, mayonnaise and seafood seasoning. Combine well
3. Add the fish to the bowl and make sure they're evenly coated
4. Place the sticks inside the air fryer and cook for 15 minutes

Cheesy Vegetable Tikka

SERVINGS - 2
CALORIES - 392, PROTEIN - 11G, FAT - 20G, CARBS - 21G

Ingredients:

- 1 tbsp olive oil
- 250g/2 cups of paneer cheese, sliced
- 200ml/1 cup of yogurt
- 1 onion, chopped
- 1 green pepper, chopped
- 1 red pepper, chopped
- 1 yellow pepper, chopped
- 1 tsp ginger garlic paste

- 1 tsp red chilli powder
- 1 tsp garam masala
- 1 tsp turmeric powder
- 1 tbsp dried fenugreek leaves
- 2 tbsp chopped coriander/ cilantro
- The juice of 1 lemon
- 8 metal skewers

Method:

1. In a large bowl, combine the garlic paste, garam masala, red chilli powder, lemon juice, fenugreek, turmeric, coriander/ cilantro and yogurt
2. Add the cheese to the bowl and make sure it is coated on all sides
3. Place in the refrigerator for 2 hours
4. Take your skewers and add the cheese, then the pepper, onion, and continue until the skewer is full
5. Add a little oil over the top
6. Repeat with the rest of the skewers
7. Place in the air fryer and cook for 15 minutes at 200C/390F

Pasta Caprese Salad

SERVINGS – 2

CALORIES – 286, PROTEIN – 19G, FAT – 12G, CARBS – 20G

Ingredients:

- 2 tbsp olive oil
- 2 tbsp balsamic vinegar
- 200g/1.5 cups of mozzarella balls
- 150g/1.2 cups of Parmesan, grated •
  150g/1.2 cups of cherry tomatoes, halved

- 1 pack of gnocchi
- 3 cloves of garlic, chopped
- 200g basil, chopped
- Salt and pepper for seasoning

Method:

1. Preheat your air fryer to 220C/420F
2. Combine the olive oil, balsamic vinegar, gnocchi, garlic, and cherry tomatoes with a little salt and pepper
3. Place the mixture inside the basket of the air fryer and cook for 10 minutes
4. Transfer the salad to a large bowl and stir in the parmesan, combining well
5. Add the basil and mozzarella and stir again

Steak & Tamari Pieces

SERVINGS - 4

CALORIES - 411, PROTEIN - 21G, FAT - 25G, CARBS - 42G

Ingredients:

- 500g/1lb steak, cut into 6 chunks
- 2 tbsp butter, melted
- 250g/2 cups of asparagus, trimmed and sliced

- 2 garlic cloves, crushed
- 75ml/0.4 cups of tamari sauce
- 3 large bell peppers, sliced
- Salt and pepper for seasoning

Method:

1. Take a zip-lock bag and add the steak and tamari sauce. Give everything a shake and close the bag
2. Place the bag into the refrigerator to rest for 1-2 hours
3. Once marinaded, remove the steaks
4. Preheat your air fryer to 250C/480F
5. Arrange the slices of asparagus and pepper in the middle of the chunks of steak then roll each piece up and use a toothpick to keep everything in place
6. Place the meat into the air fryer and cook for 6 minutes
7. Combine the melted butter with any juices that are left inside the air fryer and pour over the chunks of steak to serve

Beef Wellington

SERVINGS - 4

CALORIES - 236, PROTEIN - 35G, FAT - 22G, CARBS - 22G

Ingredients:

- 600g/1.4lb beef fillet
- 500g/1lb shortcrust pastry - if frozen, make sure it is defrosted before use
- 300g/2.5 cups of chicken liver pate
- 1 egg, beaten
- Salt and pepper for seasoning

Method:

1. Season the beef, wrap in plastic wrap and place in the refrigerator to rest for at least one hour
2. Preheat the air fryer to 160C/320F
3. Roll out the shortcrust pastry to an even thickness and brush over the edges with the beaten egg
4. Take the chicken liver pate and spread over the pastry in an even layer
5. Take the beef fillet out of the plastic wrap and place in the middle of the coated pastry
6. Wrap the pastry around the meat
7. Arrange the wellington inside the air fryer and cook for 35 minutes
8. Allow to cool slightly before slicing

Classic Enchiladas

SERVINGS – 4

CALORIES – 500, PROTEIN – 31G, FAT – 23G, CARBS – 21G

Ingredients:

- 500g/1lb minced beef
- 8 flour tortillas
- 300g/2.5 cups of coriander/ cilantro, chopped
- 1 packet of taco seasoning
- 150g/1.2 cups of sour cream

- 300g/2.5 cups of cheese, grated
- 1 can of chopped chillies
- 1 can of enchilada sauce
- 1 can of black beans
- 1 can of chopped tomatoes
- Salt and pepper for seasoning

Method:

1. Place the beef inside a frying pan and brown
2. Add the taco seasoning and combine
3. Preheat your air fryer to 200C/390F
4. Add the beef, tomatoes, beans, and the chillies to each tortilla wrap
5. Wrap up the tortillas and fold in the edges
6. Arrange cooking foil inside the air fryer and add the tortillas
7. Pour the enchilada sauce over the tortillas and the cheese
8. Cook for 6 minutes

Cheesy Taco Pie

SERVINGS – 4

CALORIES – 495, PROTEIN – 31G, FAT – 29G, CARBS – 21G

Ingredients:

- 450g/1lb ground beef or lamb – your choice
- 2 tbsp olive oil
- 4 flour tortillas
- 200g/1.5 cups of cheddar cheese, grated

- 1 garlic clove, minced
- 1 onion, chopped
- 1 tsp oregano
- 1 tsp cumin
- 112g/0.8 cups of tomato sauce

Method:

1. Take a frying pan and add the olive oil and onions over a medium heat
2. Add the meat and garlic and combine, until the beef or the lamb has browned
3. Add the cumin, oregano, and tomato sauce, stirring well and allowing to simmer for 3 minutes
4. Preheat your air fryer to 180C/350F
5. Arrange one flour tortilla into the bottom of your fryer basket
6. Add a layer of the meat and then cheese, more meat, more cheese, until all the meat has gone
7. Top with another tortilla and add any remaining cheese over the top
8. Cook for 8 minutes

Mushroom & Cheese Pasta

SERVINGS - 4

CALORIES - 410, PROTEIN - 10G, FAT - 32G, CARBS - 7G

Ingredients:

- 300g/2.5 cups of pasta, cooked
- 75g/0.3 cups of double cream/heavy cream
- 250g/2 cups of mushrooms, sliced
- 1 onion, chopped
- 70g/0.5 cups of mascarpone
- 30g/1oz parmesan, grated
- 1 tsp dried thyme
- 2 tsp minced garlic
- 0.5 tsp red pepper flakes
- Salt and pepper for seasoning

Method:

1. Combine all ingredients in a large bowl, except for the cooked pasta
2. Preheat your air fryer to 175C/347F
3. Take a 7x3" cooking pan and grease with a little oil
4. Transfer the mixture into the pan
5. Place in the air fryer and cook for 12-15 minutes, stirring after 6 minutes
6. Place the cooked pasta in serving bowls and pour the cooked mixture over the top
7. Serve with parmesan sprinkled on top

Spicy Fried Chicken

SERVINGS – 4

CALORIES – 300, FAT – 42G, PROTEIN – 19G, CARBS – 3G

Ingredients:

- 500g/17oz chicken thighs
- 1 egg, beaten
- 0.5 tsp brown sugar
- 75g/0.5 cups of flour
- 40g/0.3 cups of tapioca flour
- 180ml/0.7 cups of buttermilk

- ½ tsp paprika
- ½ tsp onion powder
- ½ tsp garlic salt
- 1 tsp garlic powder
- 0.25 tsp oregano
- Salt and pepper for seasoning

Method:

1. Preheat the air fryer to 190C/370F
2. Combine the brown sugar, paprika, onion powder, garlic powder and oregano and add the buttermilk, stirring well
3. Take a bowl and combine the tapioca flour, salt and pepper, and garlic salt
4. Take the chicken and first coat in the buttermilk mixture
5. Then, dip into the tapioca flour mixture
6. Dip into the egg and finally the flour
7. Place the chicken into the air fryer and cook for 10 minutes, until completely cooked through

Sweet Balsamic Pork Chops

SERVINGS – 4

CALORIES – 509, PROTEIN – 30G, FAT – 32G, CARBS – 30G

Ingredients:

- 4 pork chops
- 2 eggs
- 30ml/0.2 cups of balsamic vinegar
- 30ml/0.2 cups of milk
- 250g/2 cups of panko breadcrumbs
- 1 tbsp orange juice
- 250g/2 cups of pecans, finely chopped
- 2 tbsp raspberry jam
- 2 tbsp brown sugar

Method:

1. Preheat your air fryer to 200C/380F
2. Take a bowl and beat together the milk and eggs
3. Arrange the pecans and breadcrumbs in another bowl, combining well
4. Take each of your pork chops and first cover with the flour, then dip into the egg mixture, and finally the breadcrumb mixture
5. Arrange the pork chops inside the air fryer and cook for 12-14 minutes, turning halfway
6. Meanwhile, add the rest of the ingredients to a saucepan and allow to simmer for 5 minutes over a medium heat
7. Once the pork chops are cooked, pour the sauce over the top to serve

Beef in Satay Sauce

SERVINGS - 2

CALORIES - 406, PROTEIN - 20G, FAT - 12G, CARBS - 17G

Ingredients:

- 500g/1lb beef, chopped into pieces
- 2 tbsp olive oil
- 1 tbsp sugar
- 200g/1.5 cups of coriander/ cilantro, chopped
- 1 tbsp soy sauce
- 1 tsp sriracha sauce
- 1 tbsp fish sauce
- 25g/0.2 cups of roasted peanuts • 1 tbsp minced garlic
- 1 tbsp minced ginger

Method:

1. Combine the fish sauce, ginger, soy sauce, garlic, coriander/ cilantro, sriracha, olive oil and fish sauce in a bowl
2. Add the steak and coat all pieces, allowing to rest for 20-30 minutes
3. Preheat your air fryer to 200C/390F
4. Place the steak inside the fryer and cook for 9 minutes
5. Serve with the juices from the fryer and the chopped peanuts

Saucy Fish Fillets

SERVINGS - 4

CALORIES - 300, PROTEIN - 31G, FAT - 11G, CARBS - 6G

Ingredients:

- 4 fish fillets
- 2 tbsp olive oil
- 2 eggs, beaten
- 200g/1.5 cups of breadcrumbs
- 30g/0.2 cups of ranch dressing

Method:

1. Preheat the air fryer to 180C/356F
2. Place the ranch dressing and breadcrumbs into a bowl and combine well. Add the oil and mix again
3. Coat the fish in the mixture
4. Place in the air fryer and cook for 15 minutes

Jalapeño & Chicken Chimichangas

SERVINGS - 6

CALORIES - 406, PROTEIN - 21G, FAT - 22G, CARBS - 26G

Ingredients:

- 100g/0.8 cups of cooked chicken, shredded
- 150g/1.2 cups of cheese, shredded
- 6 flour tortillas
- 60g/0.4 cups of refried beans
- 1 jalapeño pepper, chopped
- 5 tbsp salsa
- 1 tsp cumin
- 0.5 tsp chill powder
- Salt and pepper for seasoning

Method:

1. Preheat the air fryer to 200C/390F
2. Take a large bowl and add all ingredients, mixing together well
3. Add 1/3 of the fill into each tortilla, rolling up and sealing the edges
4. Place inside the air fryer and cook for 7 minutes

Turkey Cutlets in Mushroom Sauce

SERVINGS - 2

CALORIES - 400, PROTEIN - 22G, FAT - 21G, CARBS - 18G

Ingredients:

- 2 turkey cutlets
- 1 can of cream of mushroom sauce
- 160ml/0.6 cups of milk
- 1 tbsp butter, melted
- Salt and pepper for seasoning

Method:

1. Preheat your air fryer to 220C/420F
2. Season your turkey cutlets and brush over with the melted butter
3. Place the cutlets inside the air fryer and cook for 12 minutes
4. Meanwhile, combine the milk and soup in a pan and cook over a medium heat for 10 minutes
5. Once the cutlets are cooked, serve with the sauce poured over the top

Exotic Chinese Pork

SERVINGS - 4

CALORIES - 286, PROTEIN - 20G, FAT - 34G, CARBS - 20G

Ingredients:

- 1 tbsp olive oil
- 450g/1lb pork loin, cut into cubes
- 1 tbsp brown sugar
- 2 tbsp soy sauce
- 1 small pineapple, cubed
- 2 tbsp toasted sesame seeds
- 75g/0.6 cups of fresh coriander/cilantro, chopped
- 1 red pepper, sliced
- 1 clove of garlic, minced
- 1 tsp ginger
- Salt and pepper for seasoning

Method:

1. Preheat the air fryer to 180C/350F
2. Take the pork loin and season with salt and pepper
3. Place all ingredients inside the air fryer basket and cook for 18 minutes
4. Serve with the sesame seeds and coriander/cilantro over the top

Jackfruit & Beans

SERVINGS - 2

CALORIES - 326, PROTEIN - 25G, FAT - 26G, CARBS - 25G

Ingredients:

- Olive oil spray
- 1 Jackfruit
- 4 wheat tortillas
- 250g/2 cup of red beans
- 100g/1 cup of pico de gallo sauce
- 50ml/0.2 cups of water

Method:

1. Take a large saucepan and add the red beans, jackfruit, pico de gallo sauce, and water, combining well
2. Bring to the boil and then turn down to a simmer, for 30 minutes
3. Preheat your air fryer to 185C/365F
4. Take a fork and mash the beans and jackfruit mixture
5. Divide the mixture evenly between the tortillas, rolling them up and folding in the edges
6. Spray each tortilla with a little oil spray and arrange inside the fryer basket
7. Cook for 9 minutes

Ginger & Garlic Cauliflower

SERVINGS – 2

CALORIES – 396, PROTEIN – 21G, FAT – 16G, CARBS – 11G

Ingredients:

- 2 tsp olive oil
- 1 tsp sesame oil
- 1 cauliflower, cut into florets
- 200ml/0.8 cups of water
- 150ml/0.6 cups of orange juice
- 3 tbsp white vinegar
- 100g/0.8 cups of brown sugar
- 200g/1.6 cups of flour
- 1 tsp minced ginger
- 2 garlic cloves, minced
- 1/2 tsp red pepper flakes
- 1 tbsp cornstarch
- 3 tbsp soy sauce
- 1 tsp salt

Method:

1. Preheat your air fryer to 220C/420F
2. Take a large bowl and add the flour, salt and water, combining well
3. Take your cauliflower and dip each floret into the bowl
4. Place the florets inside the air fryer and cook for 15 minutes
5. Place the rest of the ingredients into a saucepan
6. Bring to the boil and then turn down to a simmer for 4 minutes
7. Serve the cauliflower on a plate with the sauce over the top

EXCLUSIVE BONUS

40 Weight Loss Recipes

&

14 Days Meal Plan

Scan the QR-Code and receive
the FREE download:

AIR FRYER DESSERT RECIPES

After a busy day at work, the last thing you want to do is start grabbing multiple pans and cooking full meals. Your air fryer has you covered. You can easily make a truly sumptuous meal with your appliance, with less stress and a lot of flavour. When you add meal planning into the equation, everything becomes even easier!

Which of these fantastic air fryer dinner recipes will you try first?

Key Lime Cupcakes

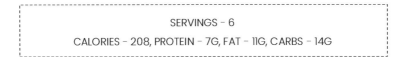

SERVINGS - 6

CALORIES - 208, PROTEIN - 7G, FAT - 11G, CARBS - 14G

Ingredients:

- 2 eggs, plus 1 egg yolk
- 200g/7oz soft cheese
- 250g/8oz Greek yogurt
- Juice and rind of 2 limes

- 60ml/0.25 cups of caster sugar
- 1 tsp vanilla essence
- 6 cupcake cases

Method:

1. Take a bowl and combine the yogurt and soft cheese until smooth
2. Add the eggs and combine
3. Add the lime juice and rind, vanilla, and caster sugar and combine again
4. Fill the cupcake cases with the mixture and allow to rest
5. Preheat the air fryer to 160C/320F 6. Place the cupcakes into the air fryer and cook for 10 minutes
6. Increase the heat to 180C/356F for another 10 minutes 8. Place the remaining mixture into a piping bag
7. Once the cupcakes have cooled, pipe the mixture on top of the cupcakes and place in the refrigerator to set

Chocolate & Vanilla Biscuits

SERVINGS - 6

CALORIES - 304, PROTEIN - 4G, FAT -16G, CARBS - 50G

Ingredients:

- 50g/1.7oz milk chocolate
- 1 egg, beaten
- 225g/7.9oz self-raising flour
- 100g/3.5oz sugar
- 100g/3.5oz butter
- 1 tsp vanilla essence

Method:

1. Preheat the air fryer to 180C/356F
2. Take a bowl and rub together the flour, butter, and sugar
3. Add the egg and vanilla, and combine to form a dough
4. Divide the dough into 6 even pieces and use your hands to form balls
5. Place in the air fryer cook for 15 minutes
6. Melt the chocolate over a pan of hot water
7. Once melted, dip the cooked biscuits into the chocolate, and allow to set

Coconut Fried Bananas

SERVINGS - 8

CALORIES - 150, PROTEIN - 20G, FAT - 21G, CARBS - 17G

Ingredients:

- 4 bananas, halved - make sure they're ripe
- 2 tbsp flour
- 2 tbsp rice flour
- 2 tbsp cornflour
- 2 tbsp desiccated coconut
- ½ tsp baking powder
- ½ tsp cardamon powder
- A pinch of salt

Method:

1. Take a bowl and add all the dry ingredients. Combine well
2. Add a little water at a time and combine to form a batter
3. Preheat the air fryer to 200C/392F
4. Line the air fryer with parchment paper and spray with cooking spray
5. Dip each banana piece in the batter mix and place it in the air fryer
6. Cook for 10 minutes, turning at the halfway point

Citrus & Chocolate Fondant

SERVINGS – 4

CALORIES – 411, PROTEIN – 14G, FAT – 37G, CARBS – 31G

Ingredients:

- The rind and juice of 1 orange
- 2 eggs
- 115g/4oz dark chocolate, melted
- 2 tbsp self-raising flour
- 4 tbsp caster sugar
- 115g/4oz butter
- 4 ramekin dishes, greased

Method:

1. Preheat the air fryer to 180C/356F
2. Take a bowl and beat the eggs and sugar until the mixture is fluffy and pale
3. Add the orange juice and rind to the melted chocolate and combine
4. Add the egg mixture and combine
5. Slowly sift the flour into the mixture and combine gently
6. Divide the mixture between the ramekin dishes
7. Place the dishes into the air fryer and cook for 12 minutes
8. Allow to cool slightly before serving

Chocolate Citrus Muffins

SERVINGS - 12

CALORIES - 600, PROTEIN - 27G, FAT - 25G, CARBS - 30G

Ingredients:

- 50ml/0.2 cups of milk
- 2 eggs
- The orange and rind of 1 large orange
- 1 tbsp honey
- 100g/3.5oz self-raising flour
- 110g/3.8oz caster sugar

- 50g/1.7oz butter
- 20g/0.7oz cocoa powder
- 1 tsp cocoa nibs
- 1tsp vanilla essence
- 12 muffin cases

Method:

1. Preheat the air fryer to 180C/356F
2. Take a bowl and combine the flour, butter, and sugar
3. Add the cocoa, vanilla honey, orange juice and rind, and mix well
4. Take another bowl and add the egg and milk together
5. Add the flour mixture and combine again
6. Add 2 tbsp of the cake batter to each muffin case
7. Place in the air fryer and cook for 12 minutes

Classic Profiteroles

SERVINGS – 9

CALORIES – 400, PROTEIN – 6G, FAT – 28G, CARBS – 30G

Ingredients:

- 6 eggs
- 100g/3.5oz butter
- 200g/7oz plain flour
- 100g/3.5oz milk chocolate
- 2 tbsp double/heavy cream, whipped

- 300ml/1.2 cups of water
- 2 tsp vanilla extract
- 50g/1.7oz butter
- 2 tsp icing sugar

Method:

1. Preheat the air fryer to 170C/338F
2. Take a medium saucepan and add the butter and water
3. Bring to the boil over a medium heat and remove once boiling
4. Stir in the flour slowly
5. Return to the heat, stirring constantly until a dough is formed
6. Slowly add the eggs and stir until the mixture is smooth
7. Create profiterole shapes with your hands out of the mixture
8. Place the profiteroles in the air fryer and cook for 10 minutes
9. Meanwhile, make the filling. Add the whipped cream (keep 2 tbsp to one side), vanilla and icing sugar to a bowl and whisk together
10. Then, create the topping by combining the butter, remaining whipped cream and butter and heating gently over a low heat until everything is melted together
11. Once the profiteroles are cool, add the filling to a piping bag and fill generously
12. Add a little of the topping and allow to set

New York Cheesecake

SERVINGS – 8

CALORIES – 800, PROTEIN – 10G, FAT – 50G, CARBS – 80G

Ingredients:

- 3 eggs
- 50ml/0.2 cups of quark
- 750g/26oz soft cheese
- 225g/7.9oz plain flour
- 100g/3.5oz brown sugar
- 100g/3.5oz butter
- 50g/1.7oz butter, melted
- 1 tbsp vanilla essence
- 250g/8oz sugar

Method:

1. Preheat your air fryer to 180C/356F
2. Take a bowl and combine the flour, sugar, and 100g of the butter
3. Use your hands to create biscuit shapes
4. Place the biscuits into the air fryer and cook for 15 minutes
5. Grease a springform tin
6. Break the biscuits up and mix with the melted butter, combining well
7. Press down into the bottom of the springform tin to make the cheesecake base
8. Mix the soft cheese and sugar in a bowl until creamy, add the eggs and vanilla and mix
9. Slowly add the quark and combine
10. Pour the cheesecake batter into the pan and coat evenly
11. Place in your air fryer and cook for 30 minutes
12. Leave the cheesecake inside the air fryer for 30 minutes to cool
13. Transfer to the refrigerator for 6 hours

Creamy Cherry Pies

SERVINGS - 6

CALORIES - 606, PROTEIN - 20G, FAT - 21G, CARBS - 27G

Ingredients:

- 75g/2.6oz cherry pie filling
- 300g/10.5oz shortcrust pastry, rolled out
- ½ tsp milk
- 3 tbsp icing sugar
- Cooking spray

Method:

1. Preheat the air fryer to 175C/347F and spray with a little cooking spray
2. Take the shortcrust pastry and use a cookie cutter to cut out 6 pie shapes
3. Add 1 ½ tbsp filling to the centre of each pie shape
4. Fold the dough over in half and seal around the edges with a fork
5. Place the pies into the air fryer and cook for 10 minutes
6. Mix icing sugar and milk together in a bowl and drizzle over the cooled pies before serving

Chocolate Soufflé

SERVINGS - 2

CALORIES - 406, PROTEIN - 21G, FAT - 27G, CARBS - 23G

Ingredients:

- 150g/5.2oz semi-sweet chocolate, chopped
- 60ml/0.25 cups of butter
- 2 eggs, separated
- 3 tbsp sugar
- ½ tsp vanilla extract
- 2 tbsp flour
- Icing sugar to serve
- 2 ramekin dishes, greased

Method:

1. Add the butter and chocolate to a saucepan and melt over a low heat
2. In another bowl beat the egg yolks, add the sugar and vanilla, and combine well
3. Slowly add the chocolate, flour, and mix well
4. Preheat the air fryer to 165C/329F
5. Whisk the egg whites to soft peaks and gently fold into the chocolate mix a little at a time
6. Add the mix to ramekins and place in the air fryer
7. Cook for 14 minutes
8. Dust with icing sugar before serving

Decadent Chocolate Cake

SERVINGS – 2

CALORIES – 503, PROTEIN – 40G, FAT – 79G, CARBS – 25G

Ingredients:

- 25g/0.8oz cocoa powder
- 3 eggs
- 75ml/0.3 cups of sour cream
- 225g/8oz flour

- 150g/5.2oz sugar
- 2 tsp vanilla extract
- ½ tsp baking soda
- 1 tsp baking powder

Method:

1. Preheat the air fryer to 160C/320F
2. Mix all the ingredients together in a bowl
3. Pour into a greased baking tin and place inside the air fryer
4. Cook for 25 minutes

Strawberry "Pop-Tarts"

SERVINGS - 12

CALORIES - 306, PROTEIN - 21G, FAT - 27G, CARBS - 20G

Ingredients:

- 75ml/0.3 cups of ice-cold water
- 100g /3.5oz strawberry Jam
- 1 tsp coconut oil, melted
- 300g/10oz whole wheat flour
- 225g/7.9oz white flour
- ¼ tsp salt
- 2 tbsp light brown sugar

- 300g/10oz icing sugar
- 2 tbsp lemon juice
- Zest of 1 lemon
- 150g/5.2oz cold coconut oil
- 1 tsp vanilla extract
- ¼ tsp vanilla extract

Method:

1. Take a bowl and combine the two flours, salt, and sugar
2. Slowly mix in the cold coconut oil
3. Add 1 tsp vanilla and 1 tbsp of the ice-cold water at a time
4. Mix until a dough is formed
5. Preheat the air fryer to 200C/392F
6. Take the dough and roll it out thinly, before cutting into 5cm x 7cm rectangles
7. Place 1 tsp of jam in the centre of half the rectangles, wet the edges place another rectangle on the top, and seal
8. Place in the air fryer and cook for 10 minutes
9. Allow to cool
10. Take a bowl and combine the icing sugar, coconut oil, lemon juice, and lemon zest
11. Top the pop tarts with the mixing and add sprinkles

Chocolate Eclairs

SERVINGS - 9

CALORIES - 200, PROTEIN - 2G, FAT -11G, CARBS - 15G

Ingredients:

- 3 eggs
- 150ml/0.6 cups of whipped cream, plus an extra 1 tbsp
- 50g/1.7oz milk chocolate
- 100g/3.5oz plain flour
- 50g/1.7oz butter, plus an extra 25g/0.8oz
- 150ml/0.6 cups of water
- 1 tsp vanilla extract
- 1 tsp icing sugar

Method:

1. Preheat the air fryer to 180C/356F
2. Take a pan and add the butter and water, allowing to melt over a medium heat
3. Remove from the heat and stir in the flour slowly
4. Return to the heat until the mix forms a single ball of dough
5. Allow to cool and then beat in the eggs until you have a smooth dough
6. Use your hands to form eclair shapes
7. Cook in the air fryer for 10 minutes and then 160C/320F for 8 minutes
8. Take another bowl and add the vanilla, icing sugar, and whipping cream until thick
9. Once cooled, fill each eclair with the cream mixture
10. Place the chocolate, 1 tbsp whipped cream, and 25g of butter in a glass bowl and melt over a pan of boiling water
11. Top the eclairs with the mixture and allow to set

Banana & Peanut Butter Bites

SERVINGS – 12

CALORIES – 396, PROTEIN – 20G, FAT – 21G, CARBS – 24G

Ingredients:

- 1-2 tsp vegetable oil
- 1 banana, sliced lengthways
- 12 wonton wrappers
- 75g/2.6oz peanut butter

Method:

1. Preheat the air fryer to 190C/374F and spray with a little oil
2. Take a wonton wrapper and add one piece of banana and a spoonful of peanut butter inside
3. Wet the edges of each wrapper and fold over to seal
4. Place in the air fryer and cook for 6 minutes

Pistachio & Pecan Brownies

SERVINGS – 4

CALORIES – 416, PROTEIN – 21G, FAT – 24G, CARBS – 20G

Ingredients:

- 75g/2.5oz flour
- 75g/2.6oz sugar
- 25g/0.8oz cocoa powder
- 75ml/0.3 cups of milk
- ½ tsp vanilla extract
- 25g/0.8oz salt
- 25g/0.8oz pecans
- 1 tbsp ground flax seeds

Method:

1. Mix all of the dry ingredients together
2. In a separate bowl, mix the wet ingredients
3. Combine both bowls until smooth
4. Preheat the air fryer to 175C/347F
5. Line a 5-inch cake tin with parchment paper
6. Transfer the brownie mixture into the cake tin
7. Cook for about 20 minutes

Fruity Nutella Sandwich

> SERVINGS – 2
>
> CALORIES – 226, PROTEIN – 17G, FAT – 20G, CARBS – 12G

Ingredients:

- 1 banana
- 2 tbsp softened butter
- 4 slices white bread
- 25g/0.8oz chocolate spread (Nutella)

Method:

1. Preheat your air fryer to 185C/365F
2. Take the bread and spread the butter on one side of each slice
3. Repeat the process with the chocolate spread, using the opposite side of each slice
4. Add sliced banana to two slices of bread then add the other slice of bread to each
5. Cut in half diagonally to form triangles
6. Place in the air fryer and cook for 5 minutes
7. Turn over and cook for another 2 minutes

Peach Pies

> SERVINGS – 8
>
> CALORIES – 406, PROTEIN – 21G, FAT – 28G, CARBS – 23G

Ingredients:

- 1 packet of shortcrust pastry
- 2 peaches, chopped
- 1 tsp cornstarch
- 1 tbsp lemon juice
- 3 tbsp sugar
- 1 tsp vanilla extract
- ¼ tsp salt

Method:

1. Take a bowl and combine the lemon juice, peaches, sugar, vanilla and salt
2. Allow to rest for 15 minutes
3. Preheat the air fryer to 180C/356F
4. Drain the peaches, retaining 1 tbsp of the juice
5. Mix the liquid with the cornstarch and mix into the peaches
6. Cut out 8x4 inch circles from the pastry
7. Add 1 tbsp of peach mix to each piece of pastry, keeping it to the centre
8. Fold the dough over to create half-moons and crimp the edges with a fork to seal
9. Spray with cooking spray
10. Place in the air fryer and cook for 12-14 minutes

Biscuit Dips

SERVINGS - 6

CALORIES - 370, PROTEIN - 4G, FAT - 14G, CARBS - 50G

Ingredients:

- 225g/1.8 cups of self-raising flour
- 50g/0.4 cups of milk chocolate, melted
- 100g/0.8 cups of butter
- 100g/0.8 cups of sugar
- 1 egg, beaten
- 1 tsp vanilla essence

Method:

1. Preheat the air fryer to 180C/350F
2. Take a bowl and rub together the butter, flour, and sugar
3. Add the vanilla and beaten egg to bring a dough together
4. Divide the dough into six equal pieces and flatten down into large cookies
5. Place in the air fryer and cook for 15 minutes
6. Dip in the melted chocolate and allow to cool before serving

Citrus & Cocoa Fondant

SERVINGS - 4

CALORIES - 400, PROTEIN - 11G, FAT - 35G, CARBS - 30G

Ingredients:

- 2 eggs
- 2 tbsp self-raising flour
- 115g/0.9 cups of butter
- 4 tbsp sugar
- 115g/0.9 cups of dark chocolate
- The rind and juice of 1 orange
- 4 ramekin dishes, greased

Method:

1. Preheat your air fryer to 180C/350F
2. Bring a pan of hot water to the boil and then place a glass dish over the top, melting the butter and chocolate together
3. Add the sugar and eggs and combine
4. Add the orange juice and rind. Combine again
5. Add the flour and fold in gently
6. Divide the mixture between the ramekin dishes and arrange inside the air fryer
7. Cook for 12 minutes

Classic Chocolate Profiteroles

SERVINGS - 9

CALORIES - 400, PROTEIN - 6G, FAT - 22G, CARBS - 27G

Ingredients:

- 200g/1.5 cups of plain flour
- 100g/0.8 cups of butter
- 50g/0.4 cups of butter
- 2 tsp icing sugar
- 6 eggs

- 2 tsp vanilla extract
- 300ml/1.2 cups of whipped cream
- 100g/0.8 cups of milk chocolate
- 300ml.0.5 cups of water

Method:

1. Preheat your air fryer to 170C/330F
2. Add the water and butter inside a saucepan and bring to the boil
3. Once boiling, remove from the heat and add the flour, stirring until you see a dough forming
4. Add the eggs and combine well
5. Create round balls (profiterole shaped) and place in the air fryer to cook for 9 minutes
6. Meanwhile, combine the whipped cream, icing sugar, and vanilla. Place to one side
7. Melt the chocolate and butter together to create the topping
8. Once the profiteroles are cooked, add the filling with a piping bag and pour the chocolate sauce over the top

Juicy Cherry Pockets

SERVINGS - 6

CALORIES - 656, PROTEIN - 20G, FAT - 23G, CARBS - 27G

Ingredients:

- Cooking spray
- 300g/0.6lb shortcrust pastry
- 75g/0.6 cups of cherry pie filling
- 0.5 tsp milk
- 3 tbsp icing sugar

Method:

1. Preheat the air fryer to 175C/340F
2. Divide the pastry into six pieces using a cookie cutter
3. Add 1.5 tbsp of the cherry pie filling to the middle of each piece of pastry
4. Fold over and use a fork to seal down the edges
5. Place in the air fryer and cook for 10 minutes
6. Combine the milk and icing sugar and drizzle over the pockets once cooled

Classic Creamy Cheesecake

SERVINGS - 8

CALORIES - 800, PROTEIN - 10G, FAT - 50G, CARBS - 87G

Ingredients:

- 225g/1.8 cups of plain flour
- 3 eggs
- 100g/0.8 cups of butter, plus an extra 100g/0.8 cups
- 100g/0.8 cups of brown sugar

- 220g/2 cups of white sugar
- 50g/0.4 cups of butter, melted
- 1 tbsp vanilla essence
- 750g/6 cups of cream cheese
- 50ml/0.2 cups of quark

Method:

1. Preheat the air fryer to 180C/350F
2. Combine the flour, brown sugar, 100g/0.8 cups of butter
3. Use your hands to create biscuit shapes and place them into the air fryer, cooking for 15 minutes
4. Meanwhile, take a springform tin and grease the inside lightly
5. Once the biscuits have cooled, use a rolling pin to break them into pieces and add to a bowl
6. Melt the remaining butter and add to the biscuit mixture, combining well
7. Press the mixture into the bottom of the springform tin
8. Combine the white sugar and cream cheese. Add the vanilla and eggs to create a smooth mixture
9. Fold in the quark and combine again
10. Transfer the mixture into the pan and smooth out into an even layer
11. Cook in the air fryer for 30 minutes
12. Allow to cool and refrigerator for at least 5 hours before serving

Old Fashioned Apple Pie

SERVINGS - 2

CALORIES - 456, PROTEIN - 21G, FAT - 27G, CARBS - 21G

Ingredients:

- 1 packet of ready-made pastry
- 2 apples, chopped
- 1 tbsp sugar, cut into cubes
- 1 tbsp butter

- 1 egg, beaten
- 2 tsp lemon juice
- 1 tsp cinnamon
- 0.5 tsp vanilla extract

Method:

1. Preheat your air fryer to 160C/320F
2. Take a baking tin and spread half the pastry over the top, trimming the edges
3. Take a bowl and combine the chopped apple, sugar, vanilla, cinnamon and lemon juice
4. Place the mixture over the pastry and add the butter cubes over the top
5. Add the rest of the pastry over the top of the pie and seal the edges. Cut three holes in the top
6. Brush the top of the pie with the beaten egg and place in the air fryer for 25-30 minutes

Traditional Soufflé

SERVINGS - 2

CALORIES - 476, PROTEIN - 21G, FAT - 27G, CARBS - 23G

Ingredients:

- 150g/1.2 cups of semi-sweet chocolate, chopped
- 3 tbsp sugar
- 2 tbsp flour
- 62g/0.3 cups of butter
- 2 eggs, separated
- 0.5 tsp vanilla extract
- 2 ramekin dishes, greased

Method:

1. Preheat your air fryer to 165C/320F
2. Take a small pan and melt the butter and chocolate together over a low heat
3. Take a separate bowl and combine the sugar, vanilla and egg whites
4. Add the chocolate mix and flour, and combine again
5. Place the eggs whites in a bowl and whisk until soft peaks appear
6. Use a spatula to gently fold the egg whites into the chocolate mixture bit by bit
7. Place the mixture inside the ramekin dishes and arrange in the air fryer
8. Cook for 15 minutes

Easy Chocolate Cake

SERVINGS - 2

CALORIES - 543, PROTEIN - 42G, FAT - 14G, CARBS - 26G

Ingredients:

- 225g/1.8 cups of flour
- 1 tsp baking powder
- 0.5 tsp baking soda
- 25g/0.2 cups of cocoa powder
- 3 eggs
- 75ml/0.7 cups of sour cream
- 150g/1.2 cups of sugar
- 2 tsp vanilla extract

Method:

1. Preheat your air fryer to 160C/320F
2. Take a large mixing bowl and combine all ingredients
3. Grease a baking tin and transfer the mixture inside
4. Cook in the air fryer for 30 minutes
5. Cool before serving

Honey & Apple Pockets

SERVINGS - 12

CALORIES - 144, PROTEIN - 4G, FAT - 6G, CARBS - 29G

Ingredients:

- Olive oil spray
- 12 empanada wraps
- 1 tsp cornstarch
- 2 tbsp honey
- 2 apples, diced

- 1 tsp cinnamon
- 1 tsp vanilla extract
- 0.25 tsp nutmeg
- 1 tsp water

Method:

1. Preheat the air fryer to 200C/390F
2. Take a medium saucepan and add the vanilla, nutmeg, honey, apples, and cinnamon inside. Cook for 3 minutes, until everything is smooth
3. Add the water and cornstarch and mix together, cooking for another minute
4. Place some of the mixture into the centre of each wrap and roll in half
5. Make sure the edges are sealed and place inside the air fryer
6. Cook for 8 minutes
7. Turn over and cook for a further 10 minutes

Banana & Walnut Bread

SERVINGS - 8
CALORIES - 170, PROTEIN - 3G, FAT - 5G, CARBS - 25G

Ingredients:

- 2 tbsp olive oil
- 2 bananas, mashed
- 2 tbsp chopped walnuts
- 2 eggs
- 75g/0.6 cups of sugar
- 200g/1.6 cups of flour
- 25g/0.2 cups of plain yogurt
- 1 tsp cinnamon
- 0.5 tsp salt
- 0.25 tsp baking soda

Method:

1. Preheat the air fryer to 155/310F
2. Take a 6" cake tin and line with parchment paper
3. Combine the cinnamon, flour, baking soda, and salt and place to one side
4. Take another bowl and combine the rest of the ingredients
5. Combine the flour mixture with the other bowl and mix together well
6. In another bowl mix together the remaining ingredients, add the flour mix and combine well
7. Pour batter into the cake tin and place in the air fryer
8. Cook for 35 minutes, turning at the halfway point

Citrus Cupcakes

SERVINGS - 6

CALORIES - 218, PROTEIN - 5G, FAT - 9G, CARBS - 11G

Ingredients:

- 250g/2 cups of Greek yogurt
- 30g/0.3 cups of caster sugar
- 200g/1.6 cups of cream cheese
- 2 eggs, plus 1 egg yolk
- Juice and rind of 2 limes
- 1 tsp vanilla essence
- 6 cupcake cases

Method:

1. Preheat the air fryer to 160C/320F
2. Combine the cream cheese and yogurt
3. Add the eggs and mix together well
4. Add the rind and lime juice, sugar, and vanilla and combine once more
5. Divide the mixture between the cupcake cases
6. Place the cupcakes in the air fryer and cook for 15 minutes

Tropical Fried Bananas

SERVINGS - 8

CALORIES - 130, PROTEIN - 21G, FAT - 19G, CARBS - 14G

Ingredients:

- 4 bananas, cut into halves
- 2 tbsp desiccated coconut
- 2 tbsp flour
- 2 tbsp cornflour
- 2 tbsp rice flour
- 0.5 tsp cardamom powder
- 0.5 tsp baking powder
- 4 tbsp water

Method:

1. Preheat your air fryer to 200C/390F
2. Place all the ingredients into a large bowl, except for the water and bananas
3. Combine well and then add a little water to create a smooth batter. You may need to add water bit by bit to get the desired result
4. Take your banana halves and dip them into the mixture, transferring to the air fryer basket
5. Cook for 5 minutes, turn over and cook for another 5 minutes

Chocolate & Orange Muffins

SERVINGS - 12

CALORIES - 630, PROTEIN - 21G, FAT - 27G, CARBS - 32G

Ingredients:

- 50ml/0.2 cups of milk
- The juice and rind of 1 orange
- 2 eggs
- 1 tbsp honey
- 110g/0.8 cups of caster sugar

- 100g/0.7 cups of self-raising flour
- 20g/0.2 cups of cocoa powder
- 50g/0.4 cups of butter
- 1tsp vanilla essence
- 12 muffin cases

Method:

1. Preheat your air fryer to 180C/350F
2. Combine the butter, sugar, and flour in a large bowl
3. Add the orange juice and rind, honey, vanilla, and cocoa and combine again
4. Take another bowl and combine the milk and egg
5. Add the egg mixture to the flour mixture and incorporate
6. Divide the batter between the muffin cases and place in the air fryer
7. Cook for 12 minutes

Smooth Banana Chunks

SERVINGS - 12

CALORIES - 356, PROTEIN - 21G, FAT - 27G, CARBS - 21G

Ingredients:

- 12 wonton wrappers
- 1-2 tsp olive oil
- 1 banana, cut lengthways
- 75g/0/6 cups of peanut butter

Method:

1. Preheat your air fryer to 190C/370F
2. Place a piece of banana and a little peanut butter inside each wonton wrapper
3. Dampen the edges of each wonton and fold
4. Arrange inside the air fryer in one layer
5. Cook for 5 minutes

Banana & Chocolate Sandwich

SERVINGS - 2

CALORIES - 250, PROTEIN - 14G, FAT - 21G, CARBS - 11G

Ingredients:

- 4 slices of white bread
- 1 banana
- 2 tbsp softened butter
- 25g/0.2 cups of chocolate spread

Method:

1. Preheat your air fryer to 185C/365F
2. Butter each slice of bread on one side
3. Cover each unbuttered side with the chocolate spread
4. Add the banana and place the slices together
5. Cut to form two triangle shapes and place inside the air fryer
6. Cook for 5 minutes
7. Turn the sandwich over and cook for a further 3 minutes

Eclairs

SERVINGS – 9

CALORIES – 220, PROTEIN – 5G, FAT – 10G, CARBS – 12G

Ingredients:

- 150ml/0.6 cups of water
- 50g/0.4 cups of milk chocolate
- 100g/0.8 cups of plain flour
- 3 medium eggs
- 150ml/0.6 cups of whipped cream, plus

- an extra 1 tbsp
- 50g/0.4 cups of butter, plus an extra 25g/0.2 cups, melted
- 1 tsp vanilla extract
- 1 tsp icing sugar

Method:

1. Preheat your air fryer to 180C/350F
2. Melt the butter and water together over a low to medium heat
3. Remove from the heat and gently stir in the flour
4. Place the pan back on the heat and stir until a dough forms
5. Remove and place to one side to cool
6. Add the eggs and beat until the dough is smooth to the touch
7. Create eclair shapes with your hands and place in the air fryer for 8 minutes
8. Place to one side to cool
9. Add the icing sugar, cream, and vanilla to a bowl and beat to form a thick consistency
10. Fill your eclairs with the mixture
11. Mix together the remaining whipped cream and melted butter for the eclair topping
12. Dip each eclair into the topping and allow to set before serving

Nutty Brownies

SERVINGS - 4

CALORIES - 401, PROTEIN - 22G, FAT - 22G, CARBS - 21G

Ingredients:

- 75g/0.6 cups of sugar
- 75g/0.6 cups of flour
- 75ml/0.3 cups of milk
- 25g/0.2 cups of cocoa powder
- ½ tsp vanilla extract
- 1 tbsp ground flax seeds
- 25g/0.2 cups of pecans
- 25g/0.2 cups of salt

Method:

1. Preheat your air fryer to 175C/340F
2. Place all the ingredients into a bowl, except for the milk, and combine well
3. Add the milk and combine to a smooth consistency
4. Take a 5" baking tin and line with parchment
5. Pour the mixture into the tin and cook for 20 minutes
6. Allow to cool before removing from the tin and slicing

Iced Strawberry Pockets

SERVINGS – 12

CALORIES – 311, PROTEIN – 18G, FAT – 21G, CARBS – 18G

Ingredients:

- 225g/7.9oz white flour
- 300g/10oz whole wheat flour
- 1 tsp coconut oil, melted
- 150g/5.2oz cold coconut oil
- 75ml/0.3 cups of cold water

- 100g /3.5oz strawberry Jam
- The zest and juice of 1 lemon
- 2 tbsp light brown sugar
- 300g/10oz icing sugar

Method:

1. Preheat your air fryer to 200C/390F
2. Combine the two flours and sugar
3. Add the cold coconut oil and combine
4. Add the vanilla and a little of the water, a bit at a time. Combine well until a dough is created
5. Roll out the dough and cut rectangles, around 5x7cm in size
6. Add a little jam in the middle of each piece and then slightly wet the edges
7. Top with another rectangle and seal the edges with a fork
8. Cook in the air fryer for 10 minutes
9. Meanwhile, combine the coconut oil, lemon zest and juice, and icing sugar
10. Top the pockets with the icing once cool

Chocolate Cookies

SERVINGS – 6

CALORIES – 300, PROTEIN – 5G, FAT – 11G, CARBS – 47G

Ingredients:

- 225g/1.8 cups of self-raising flour
- 50g/0.4 cups of milk chocolate, melted
- 100g/0.8 cups of butter
- 1 egg, beaten
- 100g/0.8 cups of sugar
- 1 tsp vanilla essence

Method:

1. Preheat your air fryer to 180C/355F
2. Rub the sugar, flour, and butter together to form breadcrumbs
3. Add the vanilla and egg and create a dough
4. Cut the dough into six pieces and create flattened balls
5. Cook in the air fryer for 15 minutes
6. Once cool, dip in the melted chocolate and leave to set

AIR FRYER SIDE RECIPES

Whether you're cooking for a special occasion or you want to spruce up dinner a little, these air fryer side recipes will add a little something extra to your lunch or dinner. Many of these side recipes also double up as snacks too!

Spicy Rice

SERVINGS – 4

CALORIES – 286, PROTEIN – 13G, FAT – 11G, CARBS – 12G

Ingredients:

- 3 tbsp olive oil
- 500ml/2 cups of chicken stock
- 500g/17oz long grain rice
- 60ml.02 cups of water
- 1 tsp chilli powder
- 1/4 tsp cumin
- 2 tbsp tomato paste

- 1/2 tsp garlic powder
- 1 tsp red pepper flakes
- 1 onion, chopped
- Half a small jalapeño pepper, de-seeded and chopped
- Salt for seasoning

Method:

1. Add a small bowl and add the water and tomato paste. Combine and place to one side
2. Take a baking pan and add a little oil
3. Wash the rice and add to the baking pan
4. Preheat the air fryer to 220C/428F
5. Add the chicken stock, tomato paste, jalapeños, onions, and the rest of the olive oil
6. Combine well and cover with tin foil
7. Place inside the air fryer and cook for 50 minutes

Avocado "Chips"

SERVINGS - 2

CALORIES - 320, PROTEIN - 9G, FAT - 18G, CARBS - 39G

Ingredients:

- 100g/3.5oz panko breadcrumbs
- 1 ripe avocado, cut into 8 slices
- 150g/5.2oz flour
- ½ tsp black pepper
- ¼ tsp salt
- 1 egg
- 1 tsp water

Method:

1. Preheat the air fryer to 200C/392F
2. Take a bowl and combine the flour, salt and pepper
3. Beat the egg and water together in another bowl
4. Add the breadcrumbs to a third bowl
5. Dip the avocado into the flour, then the egg, then into the breadcrumbs
6. Spray with cooking oil and place in the air fryer
7. Cook for 4 minutes
8. Turn the avocado and cook for a further 3 minutes

Parmesan Asparagus

SERVINGS - 4

CALORIES - 296, PROTEIN - 11G, FAT - 3G, CARBS - 12G

Ingredients:

- 1 tsp olive oil
- 1 tbsp grated parmesan cheese
- 500g/17oz asparagus
- 1 tsp garlic salt
- Salt and pepper for seasoning

Method:

1. Preheat your air fryer to 270C/518F
2. Clean the asparagus and cut off the bottom section
3. Pat dry and place in the air fryer, covering with the oil
4. Sprinkle the parmesan and garlic salt on top
5. Season to your liking
6. Cook for 10 minutes
7. Sprinkle with extra parmesan before serving

Balsamic Brussels

SERVINGS – 2

CALORIES – 100, PROTEIN – 5G, FAT – 9G, CARBS –13G

Ingredients:

- 400g/14oz Brussels sprouts, halved
- 1 tsp balsamic vinegar
- 2 tsp cooked bacon, crumbled
- 1 tbsp avocado oil
- ½ tsp salt
- ½ tsp pepper

Method:

1. Preheat your air fryer to 175C/347F
2. Take a bowl and combine the oil, salt, and pepper
3. Add the Brussels sprouts and coat well
4. Place in the air fryer and cook for 5 minutes
5. Shake and cook for another 5 minutes
6. Sprinkle with balsamic vinegar and bacon before serving

Corn on The Cob

SERVINGS – 4

CALORIES – 196, PROTEIN – 11G, FAT – 15G, CARBS – 21G

Ingredients:

- 2 ears of corn, cut into 4 pieces
- 75g/2.6oz mayonnaise
- 2 tsp grated cheese
- 1 tsp lime juice
- ¼ tsp chilli powder

Method:

1. Heat your air fryer to 200C/392F
2. Mix the mayonnaise, cheese, lime juice, and chilli powder in a bowl
3. Cover the corn in the mayonnaise mix, ensuring it is totally coated
4. Place in the air fryer and cook for 8 minutes

Herby Baby Potatoes

SERVINGS – 4

CALORIES – 100, PROTEIN – 2G, FAT – 0.3G, CARBS – 20G

Ingredients:

- 500g/17oz baby potatoes, quartered
- 1 tbsp oil
- ½ tsp garlic powder
- ½ tsp dried parsley
- 1 tsp salt

Method:

1. Preheat your air fryer to 175C/347F
2. Take a bowl and combine the oil and potatoes
3. Add remaining ingredients and combine again
4. Add to the air fryer
5. Cook for 25 minutes until golden brown. Make sure you turn halfway through

Cheesy Shishito Peppers

SERVINGS – 2

CALORIES – 256, PROTEIN – 2.5G, FAT – 3G, CARBS – 2G

Ingredients:

- ½ tbsp avocado oil
- 200g/7oz shishito peppers
- 75g/2.6oz grated cheese
- 2 limes
- Salt and pepper to taste

Method:

1. Preheat your air fryer to 175C/347F
2. Place the peppers into a bowl and mix with the oil, salt, and pepper
3. Place in the air fryer and cook for 10 minutes
4. Sprinkle with cheese before serving

Mini Aubergine (Eggplant) Bites

SERVINGS - 4

CALORIES - 200, PROTEIN - 21G, FAT - 26G, CARBS - 21G

Ingredients:

- 100g/3.5oz flour
- 2 eggs
- 1 aubergine/eggplant, sliced into ½ inch rounds
- 100g/3.5oz Italian breadcrumbs
- 50g/1.7oz grated parmesan

- 1 tsp Italian seasoning
- 1 tsp salt
- ½ tsp dried basil
- ½ tsp onion powder
- ½ tsp black pepper

Method:

1. Preheat the air fryer to 185C/365F
2. Take a bowl and combine the breadcrumbs, parmesan, salt, Italian seasoning, basil, onion powder, and pepper
3. Add the flour to another bowl, and beat the eggs in another
4. Dip the aubergine/eggplant in the flour, then the eggs, and then coat in the breadcrumbs
5. Place the aubergine in the air fryer and cook for 8 minutes
6. Turnover and cook for a further 4 minutes

Cheesy Carrot Fries

SERVINGS - 2

CALORIES - 126, PROTEIN - 27G, FAT - 22G, CARBS - 24G

Ingredients:

- 1 tbsp olive oil
- 180g/6.3oz carrots, halved
- 1 garlic clove, crushed
- 2 tbsp parmesan, grated
- Salt and pepper for seasoning

Method:

1. Preheat your air fryer to 220C/428F
2. Combine the olive oil and garlic in a bowl
3. Add the carrots to the bowl and combine again
4. Add the parmesan and make sure everything is coated in the mixture
5. Add the carrots to the air fryer and cook for 20 minutes, shaking halfway through

Spinach Stuffed Potatoes

SERVINGS - 4

CALORIES - 416, PROTEIN - 26G, FAT - 23G, CARBS - 28G

Ingredients:

- 2 large potatoes
- 50g/1.7oz spinach, chopped
- 2 tbsp nutritional yeast
- 2 tsp olive oil
- 100ml/0.5 cups of milk
- 100ml/0.5 cups of yogurt
- ¼ tsp pepper
- ½ tsp salt

Method:

1. Preheat the air fryer to 190C/374F
2. Rub the potatoes with oil and place in the air fryer
3. Cook for 30 minutes, turn and cook for another 30 minutes
4. Once cooked, cut the potatoes in half and remove the middles with a spoon
5. Mash the potato with the milk, yeast, and yogurt
6. Add the spinach, seasoning, and combine again
7. Spoon the mixture back inside the skins and return to the air fryer
8. Cook at 160C/320F for 5 minutes

Citrus & Garlic Tofu

SERVINGS - 4

CALORIES -100, PROTEIN - 6G, FAT - 10G, CARBS - 10G

Ingredients:

- 400g/14oz tofu, drained and cubed
- 2 tsp cornstarch
- 1 tbsp maple syrup
- 1 tsp orange zest
- 75ml/0.3 cups of orange juice
- 1 tbsp tamari

- 1 tbsp corn starch
- ¼ tsp pepper flakes
- 1 tsp minced ginger
- 1 tsp fresh garlic
- 75ml/0.3 cups of water

Method:

1. Place the tofu in a bowl with the tamari and combine
2. Mix in 1 tbsp cornstarch and rest for 30 minutes
3. Preheat your air fryer to 190C/374F
4. Place the remaining ingredients into another bowl and combine
5. Place the tofu in the air fryer and cook for about 10 minutes
6. Add tofu to a pan with sauce the mix and cook until sauce begins to thicken

Courgette (Zucchini) Gratin

SERVINGS - 2
CALORIES - 183, PROTEIN - 13G, FAT - 16G, CARBS - 2G

Ingredients:

- 2 courgettes/zucchinis
- 1 tbsp vegetable oil
- 1 tbsp parsley, chopped
- 4 tbsp parmesan, grated
- 2 tbsp breadcrumbs
- Salt and pepper to taste

Method:

1. Heat your air fryer to 180/356F
2. Cut each courgette in half lengthways and then cut into slices
3. Mix the remaining ingredients together in a bowl
4. Place the courgette in the air fryer and top with the breadcrumb mixture
5. Cook for 15 minutes

Salty Chickpeas

SERVINGS - 5
CALORIES - 230, PROTEIN - 6G, FAT - 8G, CARBS - 30G

Ingredients:

- 1 tbsp olive oil
- 1 can of chickpeas, drained
- 100ml/0.5 cups of white vinegar
- Salt to taste

Method:

1. Take a pan and combine the chickpeas and vinegar over a medium heat
2. Allow to simmer, remove from the heat and rest for 30 minutes
3. Preheat the air fryer to 190C/374F
4. Place the chickpeas into the air fryer and cook for 4 minutes
5. Once cooked, pour the chickpeas into an ovenproof bowl
6. Drizzle with the oil and season
7. Place the bowl into the air fryer and cook for another 4 minutes

Spicy Pickles

SERVINGS - 4

CALORIES - 170, PROTEIN - 2G, FAT - 16G, CARBS - 15G

Ingredients:

- 1 jar of dill pickle slices
- 1 egg
- 2 tbsp milk
- 50g/1.7oz flour
- 118ml/0.5 cups of mayonnaise
- 2 tsp sriracha sauce
- 50g/1.7oz cornmeal
- ½ tsp seasoned salt
- ¼ tsp paprika
- ¼ tsp garlic powder
- ⅛ tsp pepper
- Cooking spray

Method:

1. Mix the mayonnaise and sriracha together in a bowl and set aside
2. Preheat the air fryer to 200C/392F
3. Drain the pickles and pat dry
4. Mix the egg and milk together
5. In another bowl, mix all the remaining ingredients together
6. Dip the pickles into the egg mixture and then into the flour mixture
7. Spray the air fryer with cooking spray and place the pickles inside the basket
8. Cook for about 4 minutes, until crispy

BBQ Bacon Parcels

SERVINGS - 4
CALORIES - 250, PROTEIN - 20G, FAT - 30G, CARBS - 20G

Ingredients:

- 2 chicken breasts
- 7 slices of bacon, cut lengthwise and then into halves
- 200ml/0.8 cups of BBQ sauce
- 2 tbsp brown sugar

Method:

1. Preheat the air fryer to 220C/428F
2. Take a piece of chicken and wrap two strips of the bacon around it
3. Brush with the BBQ sauce and sprinkle with the brown sugar
4. Repeat with the rest of the chicken and bacon
5. Place the parcels into the air fryer basket and cook for 5 minutes
6. Turn the chicken over and cook for another 5 minutes

AIR FRYER SNACK RECIPES

Snacks aren't left out when it comes to using your air fryer. You can easily make some fantastic snacks ahead of time and use them as an add-on for your child's lunch at school, or for you and the rest of your family's work pack up too.

Of course, because your snacks are cooked in air and not oil, they're healthier, crispier, and far more delicious. You'll want to make them all!

Aubergine (Eggplant) Snacks

SERVINGS - 4

CALORIES - 180, PROTEIN - 20G, FAT - 24G, CARBS - 20G

Ingredients:

- 1 aubergine/eggplant, sliced
- 2 eggs, beaten
- 100g/0.8 cups of flour
- 50g/0.2 cups of grated parmesan

- 100g/0.4 cups of Italian breadcrumbs
- 0.5 tsp onion powder
- 1 tsp Italian seasoning
- 0.5 tsp dried basil

Method:

1. Preheat your air fryer to 185C/360F
2. Mix together the grated parmesan, basil, onion powder, Italian seasoning and breadcrumbs
3. Take the aubergine/eggplant slices and first dip into the flour, the eggs, and then the breadcrumbs
4. Cook in the air fryer for 8 minutes
5. Turn the aubergine slices over and cook for another 4 minutes

Carrot Chips

SERVINGS - 2

CALORIES - 106, PROTEIN - 21G, FAT - 21G, CARBS - 22G

Ingredients:

- 1 tbsp olive oil
- 2 tbsp parmesan, grated
- 180g/1.4 cups of carrots, cut in half
- 1 garlic clove, crushed
- Salt and pepper for seasoning

Method:

1. Preheat the air fryer to 220C/430F
2. Take a large bowl and mix the garlic and olive oil together
3. Place the carrots into the same bowl and toss to coat
4. Add the parmesan and mix everything together
5. Cook in the air fryer for 10 minutes, give the chips a shake, and cook for another 10 minutes

Hot Sauce Fried Pickles

SERVINGS - 4

CALORIES - 150, PROTEIN - 1G, FAT - 14G, CARBS - 12G

Ingredients:

- 1 jar of pickle slices, drained and dried
- 50g/0.4 cups of cornmeal
- 118ml/0.4 cups of mayonnaise
- 1 egg
- 2 tbsp milk
- 50g/0.4 cups of flour
- 2 tsp sriracha sauce
- 0.25 tsp paprika
- 0.5 tsp salt
- 0.25 tsp garlic powder

Method:

1. Preheat your air fryer to 200C/390F
2. Take a medium bowl and combine the sriracha and mayonnaise
3. Take another bowl and combine the milk and egg
4. In the next bowl add the cornmeal, flour, paprika, garlic powder, and salt
5. Dip the pickles into the egg mixture first, and then the flour
6. Place in the air fryer and cook for 4 minutes
7. Serve with the sriracha mayonnaise for dipping

BBQ Chicken Pieces

SERVINGS – 4

CALORIES – 280, PROTEIN – 21G, FAT – 32G, CARBS – 21G

Ingredients:

- 7 slices of bacon, sliced lengthwise and halved
- 2 chicken breasts
- 2 tbsp brown sugar
- 200ml/0.8 cups of BBQ sauce

Method:

1. Preheat your air fryer to 220C/420F
2. Wrap two strips of the chicken around each chicken breast
3. Spread the BBQ sauce over the top and a little brown sugar
4. Repeat with the other chicken breast
5. Place in the air fryer and cook for 5 minutes
6. Turn and cook for a further 5 minutes, ensuring the chicken is cooked through

Air Fried Chickpeas

SERVINGS - 5

CALORIES - 220, PROTEIN - 5G, FAT - 7G, CARBS - 31G

Ingredients:

- 1 tbsp olive oil
- 100ml/0.5 cups of white vinegar
- 1 can of chickpeas, drained
- Salt for seasoning

Method:

1. In a medium saucepan add the vinegar and chickpeas and warm over a medium temperature
2. Bring to a simmer and then remove the pan from the heat
3. Place to one side for half an hour
4. Preheat your air fryer to 190C/370F
5. Place the chickpeas inside the air fryer basket
6. Cook for 4 minutes
7. Add the olive oil and a little salt and combine
8. Cook for a further 4 minutes

Air Fried Avocado

SERVINGS - 2

CALORIE 300, PROTEIN - 3G, FAT - 12G, CARBS - 40G

Ingredients:

- 1 avocado, sliced
- 150g/1.2 cups of flour
- 100g/0.8 cups of panko breadcrumbs
- 1 egg, beaten
- 1 tsp water
- Salt and pepper for seasoning

Method:

1. Preheat your air fryer to 200C/390F
2. Combine the salt and pepper with the flour in a bowl
3. Take the avocado slices and dip into the flour, the egg, and finally the breadcrumbs
4. Place in the air fryer
5. Cook for 4 minutes
6. Turn over and cook for another 4 minutes

Cheesy Garlic Circles

SERVINGS - 2

CALORIES - 220, PROTEIN - 12G, FAT - 14G, CARBS - 15G

Ingredients:

- 50g/0.4 cups of parmesan, grated
- 250g/2 cups of mozzarella, grated
- 1 egg
- 0.5 tsp garlic powder

Method:

1. Combine all ingredients in a mixing bowl
2. Preheat the air fryer to 175C/340 and line with parchment paper
3. Press circles of the mixture down onto the parchment paper
4. Cook for 10 minutes

Sausage & Bacon Parcels

SERVINGS - 4

CALORIES - 273, PROTEIN - 22G, FAT - 28G, CARBS - 28G

Ingredients:

- 4 links of your favourite sausage
- 6 tbsp BBQ sauce
- 2 tbsp brown sugar
- 7 slices of bacon, sliced and halved

Method:

1. Preheat your air fryer to 220C/420F
2. Wrap some of the bacon around each link of sausage
3. Coat the top of the bacon with BBQ sauce and a little brown sugar
4. Repeat with the rest of the sausages
5. Place in the air fryer and cook for 5 minutes
6. Turn and cook for another 5 minutes

Easy Onion Bhajis

SERVINGS - 8

CALORIES - 90, PROTEIN - 2G, FAT - 12G, CARBS - 8G

Ingredients:

- 150g/1.2 cups of chickpea flour
- 4 tbsp water
- 1 red onion, sliced
- 1 onion, sliced
- 1 jalapeño pepper, minced
- 1 tsp turmeric
- 0.5 tsp cumin
- 1 clove of garlic, minced
- 1 tsp coriander
- 1 tsp chilli powder

Method:

1. Preheat the air fryer to 175C/340F
2. Mix all ingredients in a bowl and allow to sit for 5 minutes
3. Use your hands to create balls from the mixture and place in the air fryer
4. Cook for 6 minutes
5. Turn over and cook for another 6 minutes

Pork & Lime Bites

SERVINGS – 4

CALORIES – 290, PROTEIN – 15G, FAT – 20G, CARBS – 5G

Ingredients:

- 400g/14oz ground pork
- 1 tbsp Worcester sauce
- 2 tsp Thai curry paste
- 1 onion
- 1 tsp garlic paste
- 1 tbsp soy sauce
- Juice and zest of 1 lime
- 1 tsp Chinese spice
- 1 tsp mixed spice

Method:

1. Preheat the air fryer to 180C/350F
2. In a large mixing bowl, combine all ingredients until smooth
3. Use your hands to create balls
4. Place in the air fryer and cook for 15 minutes

Oozing Mozzarella Sticks

SERVINGS - 4

CALORIES - 500, PROTEIN - 29G, FAT - 26G, CARBS - 25G

Ingredients:

- 200g/1.6 cups of mozzarella, cut into strips
- 100g/0.8 cups of breadcrumbs
- 5 tbsp cornstarch
- 1 tbsp cornmeal
- 50g/0.4 cups of flour
- 60ml/0.25 cups of water
- 0.5 tsp onion powder
- 0.25 tsp oregano
- 1 tsp garlic powder
- 0.5 tsp salt
- 0.5 tsp pepper
- 0.5 tsp parsley
- 0.5 tsp basil

Method:

1. Preheat your air fryer to 200C/390F
2. Mix together the garlic powder, salt, flour, cornstarch, and cornmeal
3. Add the water and mix again
4. In a separate bowl, combine the pepper, breadcrumbs, onion powder, parsley, basil and oregano
5. Take the mozzarella strips and dip into the flour batter, followed by the breadcrumbs
6. Cook for 6 minutes
7. Turn over and cook for another 5 minutes

Easy Snack Eggs

SERVINGS - 6

CALORIES - 410, PROTEIN - 21G, FAT - 23G, CARBS - 20G

Ingredients:

- 6 eggs, boiled and shells removed
- 300g pork sausages
- 100g/0.8 cups of breadcrumbs

- 2 eggs, beaten
- 50g/0.4 cups of flour

Method:

1. Preheat your air fryer to 200C/390F
2. Lay your six sausages out on a flat surface
3. Place a boiled egg in the centre of each piece of sausage and coil the sausage around it in a circle
4. Hold it carefully and dip in the flour mixture, then egg mixture, and finally the breadcrumb mixture
5. Cook in the air fryer for 12 minutes

Carrot & Bacon Mushrooms

SERVINGS - 24

CALORIES - 50, PROTEIN - 4, FAT - 9G, CARBS - 9G

Ingredients:

- 24 mushrooms
- 2 slices bacon, chopped
- 100g/0.8 cups of sour cream
- 200g/1.6 cups of cheese, grated

- 1 green pepper, sliced
- 1 onion, diced
- 1 carrot, diced

Method:

1. Take a saucepan and cook the paper, onion, bacon, and carrot in a pan with the mushroom stalks until softened - around 6 minutes
2. Add the sour cream and cheese and combine until smooth
3. Preheat your air fryer to 175C/340F
4. Place the pepper, onion, carrot, and bacon in a pan and cook for 5 minutes
5. Stir in cheese and sour cream, cook until well combined
6. Add some of the mixture to the middle of the mushrooms and place in the air fryer
7. Cook for 7 minutes

Simple Spring Rolls

SERVINGS - 20

CALORIES - 100, PROTEIN - 3G, FAT - 3G, CARBS - 15G

Ingredients:

- 1 pack of egg roll wrappers
- 1 tbsp olive oil
- 300g/10oz ground beef
- 200g/1.6 cups of frozen vegetables
- 160g/1.2 cups of dried rice noodles,

- soaked and softened
- 1 tsp sesame oil
- 1 onion, diced
- 3 cloves garlic, crushed
- 1 tsp soy sauce

Method:

1. Cook the beef, garlic, vegetables and onion in a frying pan over a medium heat for around 7 minutes
2. Add the minced beef, onion, garlic, and vegetables and cook for 6 minutes
3. Remove the pan from the heat and add the softened noodles and soy sauce
4. Preheat your air fryer to 175C/340F
5. Add an equal strip of the mixture to each wrapper and fold over to secure
6. Brush over the middle join of the wrapper and brush with a little olive oil
7. Cook in the air fryer for 8 minutes

Jalapeño Pops

SERVINGS - 2

CALORIES - 176, PROTEIN - 10G, FAT - 21G, CARBS - 14G

Ingredients:

- 100g/0.8 cups of cream cheese
- 10 jalapeños, cut into halves with the seeds removed
- 150g/1.2 cups of breadcrumbs
- 50g/0.4 cups of parsley

Method:

1. Preheat the air fryer to 185C/360F
2. Take a bowl and combine the cream cheese with half of the breadcrumbs
3. Stir in the parsley
4. Add the mixture to the jalapeño halves and sprinkle breadcrumbs over the top
5. Place in the air fryer and cook for 8 minutes

Chilli Pakora

SERVINGS - 2

CALORIES - 156, PROTEIN - 11G, FAT - 21G, CARBS - 25G

Ingredients:

- 2 onions, sliced thinly
- 200g/1.6 cups of gram flour
- 1 tbsp crushed coriander seeds
- 0.25 tsp baking soda
- 1 tsp chilli powder
- 0.25 tsp turmeric
- Pinch of salt

Method:

1. Line the inside of your air fryer with foil and preheat to 200C/390F
2. Take a large bowl and combine all ingredients
3. Use your hands to create small balls
4. Place inside the air fryer and cook for 10 minutes, turning at the halfway point

Juicy Corn on The Cob

SERVINGS - 4

CALORIES - 180, PROTEIN - 10G, FAT - 12G, CARBS - 19G

Ingredients:

- 2 corn on the cob, halved
- 75g/0.6 cups of mayonnaise
- 0.25 tsp chilli powder
- 1 tsp lime juice

Method:

1. Preheat the air fryer to 200C/390F
2. In a bowl combine the lime juice, chilli powder, and mayonnaise
3. Dip the corn in the mixture and coat completely
4. Cook in the air fryer for 8 minutes

Jalapeño & Tomato Rice

SERVINGS - 4

CALORIES - 200, PROTEIN - 11G, FAT - 19G, CARBS - 12G

Ingredients:

- 3 tbsp olive oil
- 500g/4 cups of long grain rice
- Half a small jalapeño pepper, chopped and seeds removed
- 2 tbsp tomato paste
- 500ml/2 cups of chicken stock
- 60ml/0.2 cups of water
- 1 onion, chopped
- 1/2 tsp garlic powder
- 1 tsp red pepper flakes
- 1 tsp chilli powder
- 1/4 tsp cumin

Method:

1. Preheat your air fryer to 220C/420F
2. Combine the tomato paste and water in a bowl and set aside
3. Take a large baking pan (large enough to fit inside your air fryer) and add the oil
4. Rinse the rice and place inside the pan with the tomato paste mixture, chicken stock, onions, and jalapeños. Combine well
5. Cover the top of the pan with foil and carefully place inside the air fryer
6. Cook for 50 minutes

Brussels & Bacon

SERVINGS - 2

CALORIES - 99, PROTEIN - 6G, FAT - 10G, CARBS - 11G

Ingredients:

- 400g/3.2 cups of Brussels sprouts, halved
- 1 tbsp avocado oil
- 2 tsp bacon, cooked and crumbled
- 1 tsp balsamic vinegar
- Salt and pepper for seasoning

Method:

1. Preheat the air fryer to 175C/340F
2. Combine the oil and seasoning in a bowl and coat the sprouts well
3. Cook in the air fryer for 5 minutes
4. Shake well and cook for a further 5 minutes
5. Top with the bacon pieces and the balsamic vinegar before you serve

CONCLUSION

Now do you see how quick, easy, and truly delicious owning an air fryer can be? All of these meals and snacks are ideal for families and you'll create a much healthier lifestyle for your children as a result.

We know that air fryers cook food in air, rather than grease and fat, which means crispy, delicious, and fresher tasting food for everyone to enjoy. You might have been very surprised to see the huge range of meals you can make in an air fryer, including some seriously delicious desserts! That's the beauty of owning such an appliance.

Your air fryer should take pride of place on your kitchen worktop and you'll easily be able to access it and put it to good use whenever you feel the need - which is likely to be often!

Now you have a wealth of recipes in front of you, all that's left is to get started. Choose a recipe that calls out to you the most as your first option and then just go for it. Slowly follow the instructions and you'll notice that you become much more confident in using your air fryer after a very short while. Before you know it, you'll be a seasoned pro and telling all your family, friends, and colleagues just how amazing air fryers are!

So, choose your recipe of choice and get cooking!

EXCLUSIVE BONUS

40 Weight Loss Recipes

&

14 Days Meal Plan

Scan the QR-Code and receive
the FREE download:

DISCLAIMER

This book contains opinions and ideas of the author and is meant to teach the reader informative and helpful knowledge while due care should be taken by the user in the application of the information provided. The instructions and strategies are possibly not right for every reader and there is no guarantee that they work for everyone. Using this book and implementing the information/recipes therein contained is explicitly your own responsibility and risk. This work with all its contents, does not guarantee correctness, completion, quality or correctness of the provided information. Misinformation or misprints cannot be completely eliminated.

Printed in Great Britain
by Amazon

14470807R00087